EAST ASIAN POLITICO-ECONOMIC TIES WITH THE MIDDLE EAST

East Asian Politico-Economic Ties with the Middle East

Newcomers, Trailblazers, and Unsung Stakeholders

Shirzad Azad

Algora Publishing
New York

Library of Congress Cataloging-in-Publication Data

Names: Azad, Shirzad, 1977- author.
Title: East Asian politico-economic ties with the Middle East : newcomers,
    trailblazers, and unsung stakeholders / Shirzad Azad.
Description: New York : Algora Publishing, 2019. | Includes bibliographical
    references and index.
Identifiers: LCCN 2019037932 (print) | LCCN 2019037933 (ebook) | ISBN
    9781628944044 (trade pbk.) | ISBN 9781628944051 (hbk.) | ISBN
    9781628944068 (pdf)
Subjects: LCSH: East Asia—Relations—Middle East. | Middle
    East—Relations—East Asia. | East Asia—Foreign relations—21st
    century.
Classification: LCC DS518.14 .A93 2019 (print) | LCC DS518.14 (ebook) |
    DDC 327.5056—dc23
LC record available at https://lccn.loc.gov/2019037932
LC ebook record available at https://lccn.loc.gov/2019037933

Printed in the United States

TABLE OF CONTENTS

PREFACE

The present book sketches the Middle East policies of all players in the Northeast Asian region (henceforth East Asia), including China, Japan, South Korea, North Korea, Taiwan, and Hong Kong. Although appropriate allusions are made to contextualize some critical ancient and contemporary dynamics involving East Asia and the Middle East, the main focus of each chapter is on the relationship between the two regions over the past several years. The two sides have actually established a flurry of multifaceted connections, and their critical interactions are growing by leaps and bounds one year after another. Still, the East Asian stakeholders have adopted somewhat different approaches to dealing with their counterparts in the Middle East. This is a major reason why the policy of each player and the relevant issues are tackled in a separate chapter. In organizing chapters, moreover, divisions are made based on the relative status and weight of each East Asian player in the Middle East (i.e., prioritizing a more powerful country over a less influential player).

Chapter 1, therefore, gives prominence to China's approach to the Middle East during the leadership of Xi Jinping. The presidency of Xi Jinping ushered in a new era in Chinese foreign policy toward the Middle East. "Striving for achievement" emerged generally as Xi's policy toward the outside world as a whole, and the region could potentially offer enormous opportunities in serving as a testing ground for this new approach.

China's paramount leader, moreover, announced the "One Belt, One Road" (OBOR) initiative, or "Belt & Road Initiative" (BRI), with a special priority given to the Middle East. The stakes became quite high as the Chinese needed to simultaneously deal with a whole host of other sophisticated and resourceful stake-holders in this complex region. As a consequence, China's drive toward playing the role of a neutral, nonpartisan great power eventually led to some constructive as well as confusing patterns of policy behaviors with regard to different developments in different parts of the region as outlined in the first chapter.

In Chapter 2, the main focus is about the significance of Shinzo Abe's initiatives to boost his Asian country's Mideast credentials. With his frequent travels to the Middle East, more than all other Japanese top leaders in the past, Shinzo Abe had been destined to play a distinctive role in redefining Japan's foreign policy approach toward the region. Essentially, when Abe returned to power in late 2012, he succeeded to establish a relatively stable and long-term government which strived to reappraise some contentious elements of Tokyo's internal and external policies. Reassessing Japan's conventional low-profile orientation to the Middle East was particularly a major objective of the Abe government because the region had turned out to be closely and dubiously connected to some pivotal political and security reforms which Abe and his committed coterie of stout-hearted adherents had long pursued domestically. By doubling down Japan's political engagement in different parts of the Middle East, therefore, Abe took advantage of what his country had capitalized in the region in more recent times to especially accelerate the accomplishment of some other political and security aspirations he favored ardently.

Chapter 3 appraises South Korea's dream of another Middle East boom like the one that sparked to life under the truncated presidency of Park Geun-hye. In spite of her troubled presidency at home and a premature, ignominious exit from power, Park Geun-hye made serious attempts to bolster the main direction of the Republic of Korea's (ROK) foreign policy toward the Middle East. A collaborative drive for accomplishing a new momentous boom was by and large a dominant and recurring theme in the Park government's overall approach toward the region. Park enjoyed both personal motivation as well as politico-economic justifications to push for such arduous yet potentially viable objective. Although the ROK's yearning for a second boom in the Middle East was not accomplished under the Park presidency, nonetheless, the very aspiration played a significant role in rekindling and initiating policy measures in South Korea's orientation toward different parts of a greater Middle East region, extending from the Gulf Cooperation Council (GCC) to Morocco.

In Chapter 4, the key argument is how a change in the top leadership of North Korea could inevitably influence the dynamics of Pyongyang's orientation toward the Middle East almost since the mid-1990s onward. In fact, North Korea has been in fairly close contact with the Middle East on and off for more than six decades. In spite of its relatively low-profile and widely misperceived presence in the region, however, the nature and scope of the communist East Asian state's connections to various parts of the Middle East have never remained standstill or unidirectional. Quite to the contrary, a combination of external, and especially internal, elements have pushed North Korea to expand the number of its Mideast partners as well as different areas of interactions beneficial to both sides. This process has gained momentum under the second and third generations of the top political leadership in Pyongyang no matter if many in the world may still have a sneaking suspicion about its increasingly normalizing relationship with the region.

Chapter 5 explores Taiwan's often invisible presence in the Middle East. In spite of its peculiar international standing and regardless of its geographical distance as well as politico-cultural differences with the Middle East, nonetheless, Taiwan has surprisingly managed to forge manifold connections to the region for close to seven decades. From building amicable and symbiotic politico-diplomatic ties with key Mideast countries to being in continuous partnership with them without the privilege of having those instrumental types of attachment, therefore, Taipei has certainly occupied a unique position in the international relations of East Asia–Middle East. Still, such anomaly has largely escaped the attention of both academic and policy circles around the world, and that is why major developments in Taiwan's interactions with the Middle East over the past several decades are hardly enough recorded or scrutinized. This chapter aims to make up partially for such critical shortcoming by probing Taiwan's atypical foreign policy orientation toward the Middle East through focusing on some critical ups and downs in Taipei's political, economic, technological, cultural, and even military connections to the region.

Lastly, Chapter 6 looks into some important issues in Hong Kong's connections to the Middle East. The port city of Hong Kong has played a crucial role in a whole host of commercial and financial interactions between East Asia and the greater Middle East region over the past several decades. Even when Hong Kong became an integral part of China in 1997, the Special Administrative Region (SAR) continued to grease the wheels of the multifaceted relationship between the East Asian countries, China in particular, and their partners throughout the Middle East. Besides its conventional function in smoothing the way for economic and financial ties, moreover, the SAR is increasingly contributing to cultural and recreational activities involving the two regions; interesting matters which are tackled in the final chapter of this study.

Shirzad Azad
Shanghai

CHAPTER 1. CHINA IN THE MIDDLE EAST: ASPIRING TO BECOME A GREAT POWERBROKER

After decades of trial and error, the Chinese seem to have become more self-assured about the direction of their Middle East approach. They have considerably expanded their engagement by embarking upon new strategies reflecting China's omnidirectional orientation to the wider Middle Eastern environment. And in sharp contrast to its previously lackluster record in the region, moreover, China proclaims rather assertively that it "has never been an onlooker in Middle Eastern affairs."[1]

It was not long ago that the Chinese were perpetually looking for an excuse to sidestep any deep and dangerous involvement in the Middle East. Chinese officials and specialists astutely saw the region as a "graveyard of great powers" and simply beyond China's immediate interests. Even when China was being urged hard by other stakeholders to play a "constructive role" in a Middle Eastern affair, they were firm in swiftly ditching such inconvenient ideas by accentuating their "ignorance and incompetence" about the region.

More important than a change in tone and rhetoric, however, the nature and scope of the Chinese relationship with the Mid-

---

1 "Waijiao bu: Zhongguo zai zhongdong shiwu shang conglai dou bushi 'kanke'" [Foreign Ministry: China Has Never Been 'Onlooker' in Middle East Affairs], *Xinhua*, March 22, 2017.

dle East have evolved significantly. From the end of the Korean War in 1953 almost until the early 1980s, China's involvement in the Middle East was largely ideological and political, without either strong emotional attachment or significant physical presence. Still, a great deal of this had to do with Beijing's fierce competition with the then Soviet Union.[1] As the Chinese ventured in earnest into their open-door and reform policies, they gradually and quietly abandoned their politico-ideological emphasis in the Middle East by capitalizing more and more on potential economic and financial opportunities. In fact, this "money in command mantra" of the reform era was a calculated low-key strategy that continued almost until the end of Hu Jintao's presidency in March 2013.[2]

Under the leadership of Xi Jinping, however, the Chinese are obsessively striving to distance themselves from the foregoing unidirectional overtures toward the Middle East. By taking bold initiatives and persuading their counterparts in the region to forge all-out connections which would eventually serve the two sides, the Chinese are hell-bent on discarding their quondam proclivities toward the region. China has clearly demonstrated that it is now engaging the region in strategic and political as well as in economic and cultural realms. This new approach is also, as the Chinese often firmly asserts, devoid of the ideological streaks or the solely economic objectives that characterized earlier periods. On top of that, the Chinese insist that their recent Middle East orientation is spontaneous and creative since it is diametrically opposed to their previous apathetic and reactive approach. What then does the Chinese approach to the Middle East under Xi Jinping look like, and how does it play out in different parts of the region?

The One Belt, One Road enterprise: A panacea for all Middle East ills

As the head of a new generation of leadership, Xi Jinping has turned out to be a maverick of a sort in the history of Chi-

---

1 John F. Copper, "Chinese Objectives in the Middle East," *China Report* 5 (January–February 1969), pp. 8–13.

2 "Zhongguo zai zhongdongde xinjuese" [China's New Role in the Middle East], *Xinhua*, January 15, 2016.

nese Communist Party (CCP) which has ruled China for some seven decades. He virtually became the first of China's patrician princelings to rule the roost in Chinese politics. Xi came from a different background and swiftly gave his wife a dazzling, unprecedented role in public life, but far more important was a set of critical agenda items that he and his team unexpectedly incorporated into China's domestic and foreign policies.[1] In domestic politics he introduced the "Chinese Dream" (*zhongguo meng*), which consists of new economic and social schemes to make China a better place for its citizens.[2] With regard to foreign policy, China was now to move from "keeping a low profile" (*tao guang yang hui*) toward "striving for achievement" (*fenfa youwei*).[3] The "striving for achievement" agenda was still going to be achieved through a whole host of initiatives the Xi team made known subsequently.[4]

Among all the plucky initiatives related to foreign affairs, however, nothing was more pivotal than the "One Belt, One Road" (OBOR or *yidai yilu*) plan, also known as the Belt and Road Initiative (BRI). As the main plank of Xi Jinping's foreign policy, the OBOR formed the nucleus of various strategies which were to supply grist to the mills of Chinese drive toward achievement beyond its frontiers. In order to help China move through the

1 David M. Lampton, *Following the Leader: Ruling China, from Deng Xiaoping to Xi Jinping* (Berkeley and Los Angeles, CA: University of California Press, 2014), p. 27.

2 In the words of one observer, "In China, communism and socialism are slogans, religion is represses, and democracy is not allowed. So what flourishes is mostly materialism." Richard Haass, *War of Necessity, War of Choice: A Memoir of Two Iraq Wars* (New York: Simon & Schuster, 2009), p. 179.

3 Of course, the Xi team's obsession with foreign affairs, particularly its embarkation on costly projects such as the "One Belt, One Road" initiative and large aid packages to poor countries in Africa, has come under sever criticisms by many inside the Chinese society. The critics want the Chinese government to pay more attention to China's dire domestic problems instead of spending its resources to sort out the troubles of other nations. "Who Is Chinese Professor Wenguang Sun?" *Voice of America*, August 2, 2018; and "A Chinese Professor was Ominously Forced Off-air after Police Broke into his Home during an Interview Criticizing the Government," *Business Insider*, August 3, 2018.

4 Howard W. French, *Everything Under the Heavens: How the Past Helps Shape China's Push for Global Power* (New York: Alfred A. Knopf, 2017), pp. 19–20.

gears successfully, the crucial role of the OBOR design had to be ineluctably accentuated in every possible way.[1] Besides a proactive participation of the East Asian country's media and press, the Chinese officials and institutions both in public and private sectors all were also given an optimal opportunity to make their pitch. From conveying international conferences to arranging courts of adjudication and from offering academic scholarships to hosting publicity exhibitions, therefore, the Chinese under Xi left no stone unturned in an effort to vouchsafe a successful outcome of the OBOR agenda. Even in the heydays of Maoism, China had probably never engaged in such a passionately nationwide campaign to promote a certain foreign policy objective throughout the world.[2]

The initial idea behind the OBOR project was to revive the glorious memory and function of the ancient Silk Road. While the old Silk Road used to be a multinational, multi-pronged, and multi-purpose venture, the Chinese simply ignored their previous partners and unilaterally coined the OBOR (*yidai yilu*) term. A string of nations and regions had previously contributed enormously to that trajectory, while many in China now wanted to hog all the glory. They soon became more ambitious, carving out several versions of this mega project such as ground Silk Road, maritime Silk Road, aerial Silk Road, polar Silk Road, etc.[3] Experts and pundits from all walks of life, moreover, evaluated the strategic and political as well as economic and cultural ramifications of this Chinese grand design which is going to cover some 66 countries with a combined population of around 4.4 billion people across the world. Some in the United States and

---

1 "Zhongguo zhongdong wenti teshi: 'Yidai yilu' jiang chengwei zhongdong heping jincheng zhongyao zucheng bufen" [Chinese Special Envoy to the Middle East: 'One Belt One Road' to Become an Important Part of the Middle East Peace Process], *Xinhua*, April 6, 2015.

2 "Belt and Road Plays Key Role in Joint Terror Fight," *Global Times*, July 12, 2017; and "B&R Can Transcend Clashes of Civilizations," *Global Times*, July 23, 2017.

3 Tom Miller, *China's Asian Dream: Empire Building along the New Silk Road* (London: Zed Books, 2017); "China Says no Geopolitical Consideration in its Role in Middle East," *Xinhua*, April 14, 2017; and "China: We are a 'Near-Arctic State' and we Want a 'Polar Silk Road'," *CNBC*, February 14, 2018.

Europe considered the OBOR initiative to eventually threaten certain Western interests here and there,[1] while others in India dubbed the whole project a bold move of "Chinese imperialism."[2] Whether or not such assessments and appraisals stemmed from national jealousy or political realism, the OBOR scheme, based on what the Chinese advertised, had been destined to effect the lives of many people in different parts of the world, including the greater Middle East region.[3]

There has been hardly a single policy or presentation on the OBOR initiative in which the Chinese have not given prominence to the role of the Middle East in a successful implementation of their giant project. In fact, the Middle East occupies a unique place in the OBOR scheme pretty much similar to what the region contributed to the ancient Silk Road.[4] Not only the Middle East lies at the very heart of this huge Chinese enterprise (its ground route in particular) stretching across the giant landmass of the Eurasian continent, it is this region that could eventually make it or break it for China.[5] Unlike most of their

---

1 "Why China's 'One Belt, One Road' Plan is Doomed to Fail," *South China Morning Post*, August 6, 2016; "Assessing Chinese Imperialism: How China will Use the One Belt, One Road," *The Washington Times*, September 19, 2017; "China's Belt and Road a Dilemma for Germany," *Asia Times*, June 1, 2018; and "US Competes with China's 'Belt and Road Initiative' with US$113 Million Asian Investment Programme," *South China Morning Post*, July 30, 2018.

2 "US Backs India's Opposition to China's One Belt, One Road Initiative," *Hindustan Times*, October 4, 2017; "No Change in India's Position on China's Belt and Road Initiative: MEA," *Hindustan Times*, April 6, 2018; and "U.S.-Led Infrastructure Aid to Counter China in Indo-Pacific," *Bloomberg*, July 31, 2018.

3 "Belt and Road Can 'Solve Global Woes'," *Global Times*, May 3, 2017; "Mosallas Tehran, Moscow va pekan batelossehr tamam doshmanihay gharb ast" [The Triangle of Tehran, Moscow and Beijing Nips in the Bud All Western Animosity], *Kayhan*, January 24, 2018, p. 1; and "Belt and Road will Boost Ties with Middle East," *China Daily*, January 26, 2018.

4 "For China, the Belt and Road Run through the Middle East," *South China Morning Post*, July 14, 2018.

5 Dennis Bloodworth and Ching Ping Bloodworth, *The Chinese Machiavelli: 3000 Years of Chinese Statecraft* (New Brunswick and London: Transaction Publishers, 2009); and Robert G. Sutter, *U.S. Policy Toward China: An Introduction to the Role of Interest Groups* (Lanham, MD: Rowman & Littlefield, 1998), pp. 39–40.

Western and Eastern counterparts, moreover, many Middle East countries have by and large jumped on the bandwagon in support of the Chinese mega plan. They have been upbeat about the true intentions of China with regard to the OBOR, promising to do all they could afford in the materialization of the Chinese project.[1] Indeed, part of such optimism and willingness derives from the way the Chinese have promoted their grand program across the region.

The logic through which the Chinese have publicized their OBOR has virtually connected the grand project to all Middle Eastern advantages and disadvantages.[2] While the Middle East's strategic location and resources, as the Chinese often argue enthusiastically, are very vital to the implementation of the OBOR, the region's chronic problems would be cured equally and successfully through various phases of this China-initiated project. Like a bolt from the blue, therefore, the Chinese OBOR plan has come to the rescue, offering appropriate solutions for the Middle East's serious ills. As a panacea of sorts, the OBOR initiative is a timely antidote for the region's politico-ideological maladies as it is comparably a good remedy for its economic and social malaises. This is a general picture of how the Chinese under Xi have skillfully made close links between their grand foreign policy initiate (i.e., the OBOR plan) and its positive outcomes for the Middle East.[3] In spite of this overall approach, China's interests in different parts of the region and its strategies to safeguard those pivotal interests have never been identical.

---

1 "Zhongdong gejie dui zhongguo chongman qidai" [Middle East Full of Expectations from China], *Xinhua*, January 24, 2016; and "Wang Yi: Zhongguo zai zhongdong fahui zuoyong meiyou diyuan zhengzhi kaolu" [Wang Yi: China not after Geopolitical Consideration in the Middle East], *Zhonghua renmin gongheguo waijiao bu* (PRC's Ministry of Foreign Affairs), April 13, 2017.

2 "'Yidai yilu' changyi huiji zhengge zhongdong" ['One Belt One Road' Benefits the Entire Middle East], *Xinhua*, May 9, 2017; "Xi Jinping's Marco Polo Strategy," *Project Syndicate*, June 12, 2017; and "Belt and Road Positive Force for Middle East," *China Daily*, August 1, 2018.

3 "Ri mei: Zhongguo zai zhongdong yi quanmian wancheng zhanlue bushu" [Japanese Media: Chinese Strategic Deployment in the Middle East Almost Complete], *Duowei Xinwen*, November 6, 2017.

Iran: The cynosure of all Chinese initiatives

China had long designated Iran a key member of its coalition of "like-minded partners," and Xi's belt and road initiative was to only augment the Iranian status in Beijing's broader strategic calculations. Iran used to be a pivotal depot in the ancient Silk Road as the country made indispensable contributions to critical commercial and cultural exchanges taking place on that renowned route. In the same way, the Iranian position could play a very significant role in achieving some major objectives the Chinese had thoughtfully and strategically designed for the modern version of the Silk Road.[1] In fact, if the greater Middle East region was to be the hub of China's OBOR project, Iran would virtually function as the nub of this hub.[2] That is why in a number of high-profile policy and academic meetings the Chinese under Xi needed to make overtures to their Iranian counterparts with regard to the justification for and necessity of Sino–Iranian cooperation toward the realization of the OBOR aspirations,[3] though luckily for China there happened to be few fierce skeptics and staunch anti-OBOR voices in Iran as compared to many other parts of the world.[4]

Meanwhile the first year of Xi Jinping's presidency coincided with Iran's determination to chip away at its international troubles by agreeing to negotiate over finding a long-lasting solution

---

1 James A. Millward, *The Silk Road: A Very Short Introduction* (New York: Oxford University Press, 2013), pp. 49–53; and Robert D. Kaplan, *The Revenge of Geography: What the Map Tells Us About Coming Conflicts and the Battle against Fate* (New York: Random House, 2012), pp. 42, 166, 194.

2 "Iran's Role in New Silk Road Emphasized," *Financial Tribune*, May 17, 2017; and "China's Push to Link East and West Puts Iran at 'Center of Everything'," *The New York Times*, July 25, 2017, p. A9.

3 Shirzad Azad, "Mutual Strategic Ambiguity: A Cautious Iranian–Chinese Approach to the Realization of the 'One Belt, One Road' Initiative," *International Symposium on China–Iran Cultural Communication and "One Belt, One Road Initiative": Conference Manual*, Chinese Academy of Social Sciences, Beijing, September 4–5, 2017, pp. 102–108.

4 "'Yidai yilu' kaita zhongyi hezuo xinkongjian" ['One Belt One Road' Provides a New Ground for Sino–Iranian Cooperation], *Xinhua*, January 19, 2016; and "Zhuyilang dashi: Zhong yilang guozai 'yidai yilu' kuangjia xiade hezuo" [Ambassador to Iran: Sino–Iranian Cooperation under 'One Belt One Road' Initiative], *Renmin Ribao* (People's Daily), June 1, 2017.

for the nuclear controversy. This issue provided fortuitously a unique opportunity for China to put into test Xi's *fenfa youwei* vision. As a major stakeholder in the P5+1 group (the United States, Russia, France, Britain, China, and Germany), the Chinese under Xi had certainly found a propitious occasion to practice their tempting leitmotif of "striving for achievement" on the world stage. The protracted negotiations, which lasted for some eighteen months, helped China to chalk up point after point for its diplomatic and political maneuvers; it was a promising time to shine within the prestigious club of great powers, contribute to peace and prosperity in the Middle East by settling one of its menacing problems, and prove how Beijing could be a "constructive partner" for Tehran in hard times. These significant achievements subsequently made China more adamant in opposing the Trump administration's desire to pull out of the hardly-gained landmark nuclear deal with Iran.[1]

The Chinese active participation in the negotiations over the Iranian nuclear program and the ensuing deal had obviously many advantages for China, but the whole episode was not really devoid of any downside for the East Asian power. China was particularly anxious about the impact of the nuclear deal on its economic interests in Iran. After all, the Chinese had been envied by many in the West and the East for winning big in the wake of a regime of sundry sanctions levied against Iran because of its allegedly nuclear program.[2] China's major international competitors had been railroaded into a tough decision of retreat from Iran, providing a better ground for many Chinese companies to benefit greatly from the bustling Iranian markets.[3] As a case in

---

1 "China Fights for Iran Deal to Fulfill Its own Geo-economic Interests," *Mercator Institute for China Studies*, January 16, 2018; "Quitting Iran Deal will Jeopardize Regional Stability," *Global Times*, April 3, 2018; and "Russia, China Denounce U.S. Efforts to Change Iran Deal, World Trade Rules," *Radio Free Europe/Radio Liberty*, April 6, 2018.

2 "Suestefadeh kharejiha az bazaar Iran" [Exploitation of Iranian Market by Foreigners], *Jahan Sanat*, June 1, 2017, pp. 1, 12; "Nixing the Iran Deal Would be a Boon to China," *Axios*, April 4, 2018; and "China Poised to Profit as Europe Companies Feel Iran Pain," *Financial Times*, May 9, 2018.

3 Andrew J. Nathan and Andrew Scobell, *China's Search for Security* (New York: Columbia University Press, 2012); p. 177.

point, the two-way Iranian–EU trade tumbled from nearly $33 billion in 2007 to around $22.5 billion in 2017, while the Iranian–Chinese commercial interaction for the same period ratcheted up from some $16 billion to more than $37 billion.[1] As compared to what major Western European countries had experienced in Iran in the wake of the economic sanctions, the net loss for the Japanese as well as the Americans was much more significant.[2]

In order to better vouchsafe its ever-expanding economic, beyond its politico-strategic, interests in Iran, therefore, Xi Jinping became the first Chinese top leader in about 14 years to embark upon a high-profile visit to Tehran in January 2016. Accompanied by a relatively large entourage of political and business officials, Xi's trip was intended to get assurance from the Iranians that the nuclear deal and Iran's somewhat improved relations with the West, the EU in the particular, were not to come at the cost of China (though a number of Iranian officials had already assured Beijing of this.[3] Moreover, during Xi's meetings in Tehran, the two countries seemingly out of the blue started

---

1 "Nixing the Iran Deal Would be a Boon to China," *Axion*, April 4, 2018.

2 In spite of the fact that the international regime of sanctions played an indispensable role both in the penetration and promotion of Chinese interests in Iran particularly during the past decade, however, the Chinese from the public and private sectors keep reminding their Iranian counterparts that they "greatly assisted" them in those tough days and austere conditions. The Chinese not only refrained to provide the Iranians with whatever technological and financial helps Iran required then, they often charged them handsomely for any type of typical technology or normal service the Iranian asked for. China has simply strived to often use the "timely assistance" delusion as a bargaining chip in its relationship with Iran in the post-sanctions era, while the bitter truth is that the Chinese by and large took advantage of those special circumstances and primarily enriched themselves at the cost of their Iranian counterparts. Indeed, it is China under a new generation of predatory and covetous "communists," and definitely not Iran under the visionary Islamic Republic, that has become the poster child for engaging in exploitative commercial interactions with susceptible partners across the world and taking advantage fully of their troubles and misfortunes, one way or the other. For more details see: Shirzad Azad, *Iran and China: A New Approach to Their Bilateral Relations* (Lanham, MD: Lexington Books, 2017), pp. 47–67.

3 "Yilang yanzhongdi meiguo: Ruhe cong tianshi bian cheng mogui?" [United States in the Eyes of Iran: How It Changed from Angel to Devil?], *Xinhua*, April 12, 2012; and "Duanjiao fengbo shi ting yilang ru shang he zhongguo zhandui?" [Can Iranian Jump on Chinese Team Turn Off the Turmoil?], *Duowei Xinwen*, June 7, 2017.

to discuss the prospect of increasing their trade turnover from less than $40 billion to $600 billion.[1] Such a high volume of commercial exchange would turn Iran into China's biggest trading partner in the Middle East.[2]

Although no one explained how they were going to achieve such an ambitious goal, the lofty figure had a lot to do with China's OBOR calculations. Besides having solidified their unique position as Tehran's largest trading partner a decade earlier, the Chinese had already become one of Iran's top international investors by pouring in billions of dollars to build the country's new infrastructure projects, ranging from railways and highways to power plants and ports. The funds earmarked to finance various OBOR initiatives in Iran were certainly an effective step toward realizing the $600 billion trade goal. Iran was at the mercy of China for cash and credits, but it also needed Chinese technology to meet its insatiable domestic needs.[3]

Another very critical factor was China's distinctive position as the top destination for Iran's non-oil exports. Many years of national isolation and international sanctions had taken a heavy toll on foreign markets for Iranian non-energy exports.[4] Most of Iran's top trading partners were no longer able or willing to purchase a significant part of Iranian non-oil goods, so the country had to rely on China as a major customer for its non-energy exports.[5] China is a giant market and would comfortably absorb a significant share of the Iranian commodities besides energy

1 "Saderat Iran be chin dar sal 2017" [Iran's Exports to China in 2017], *Tabnak*, February 6, 2018.

2 "Asgaroladi matrah kard: Iran bozorgtarin sharik tejari chin dar khavarmyaneh" [Asgaroladi Stated: Iran Largest Trading Partner of China in the Middle East], *Eghtesad-e Melli*, April 8, 2018, pp. 1, 9.

3 "'Zhongguo zhizao' zai yilang zhanfang guangcai ['Made in China' Shines Brightly in Iran], *Xinhua*, January 22, 2016; and "China Remains Iran's Top Trade Partner," *Financial Tribune*, April 15, 2018.

4 Michael Moran, *The Reckoning: Debt, Democracy, and the Future of American Power* (New York: Palgrave Macmillan, 2012), p. 226.

5 "BRICS Accounts for One-Third of Iran's Non-Oil Trade," *Financial Tribune*, December 5, 2017; and "Asian Countries – Main Destination of Iran's Non-oil Exports," *Trend News Agency*, December 26, 2017.

products.[1] The Chinese market is going to become even more pivotal as Iran is belatedly shoring up its domestic industries and national brands. Epitomized by naming the solar calendar year of 1397 (2018–2019) as the "Year of Support for Iranian Products,"[2] the Islamic Republic's recent champion for economic development and job creation would further facilitate the way for the Chinese to meet the needs of their Iranian counterparts in many financial, technological, commercial, and even educational fields.

In spite of all substantial emphasis put on the politico-strategic and economic parameters in the Sino–Iranian relationship, nonetheless, culture and cultural methods became a new means of strengthening Chinese long-term position in Iran. Successive Chinese governments in the past several decades had obviously not been ignorant totally of the role of culture in Beijing's growing connections to Tehran.[3] But China under Xi Jinping seemed to be more cognizant about soft power and the promotion of cultural activities in advancing Chinese critical interests in different parts of the world, including the "old friend" *(laoyou)* Iran.[4] One particularly important area of attention was the lobby for setting up a more number of Confucian institutes in major bodies of higher education in Iran.[5] Regardless of its "non-

---

1 Thomas Juneau and Sam Razavi, *Iranian Foreign Policy since 2001: Alone in the World* (Abingdon and New York: Routledge, 2013); and "Iran to Help India Make an End-run around China and Pakistan," *Nikkei Asian Review*, February 17, 2018.

2 The solar calendar year of 1398 (2019–2020) is called the "Year of Boosting Production" or the "Year of the Production Boom."

3 "Expert Says B&R Initiative Can Boost China's Soft Power," *China Daily*, August 21, 2017.

4 "Zhongguo yu yilang de guanxi" [The Sino–Iranian Relationship], *Renmin Ribao* (People's Daily), June 30, 2011; "Zhongguo yu yilang: Lijing kaoyan de 'laoyou'" [China and Iran: Proven 'Old Friends'], *Xinhua*, January 21, 2016; and "Mosallas talaee Iran, rusiyeh va china America ra be zanoo darmiavarad" [The Golden Triangle of Iran, Russia and China Would Bring the United States to Its Knees], *Kayhan*, December 6, 2016, p. 1.

5 "Avvalin shoebeh moasseh Confucius dar Iran goshayesh yaft" [First Branch of Confucius Institute Opened in Iran], *Hamshahri Online*, January 14, 2009; "Doorkhiz chin baray kasb ghodrat narm ba pool" [China Strives to Achieve Soft Power with Money], *Taadol Newspaper*, December 29, 2014; and "Reshteh zaban va adabiat chini dar daneshgah Tehran rahandazi shod" [Discipline of Chinese Language and

profit" and "independent" trappings, a Confucian Institute is certainly supported and financed partially, if not wholly, by the government of China in order to serve the East Asian country's interests in various forms.[1] This cultural strategy of the Chinese government dovetailed neatly with a more recent step taken by the Iranian government to pay closer attention to the field of Chinese studies by launching, albeit belatedly, several academic departments on the Chinese language and research at a number of top national institutions of higher education especially those located in the metropolitan city of Tehran.

The GCC: The OBOR tallies with the 2030 Vision

Over the past several years, the Gulf Cooperation Council (GCC) has undergone significant developments domestically, regionally, and internationally. After some three decades of functioning as a rather united and purposeful regional body, the GCC all of a sudden encountered turbulent circumstances which seriously threatened its very survival. Even when the Arab body was teetering on the brink of disintegration, however, the Chinese under Xi heedfully refrained from taking any politico-diplomatic position inimical to the core interests of either a GCC member or a major stakeholder outside the regional bloc.[2] For the Chinese government, the unprecedented troubles within the GCC were simply an internal affair of the Arab bloc and beyond China's "hands-off" approach toward the region. By walking a tightrope of diplomatic bafflegab, moreover, the East Asian country strived to maintain, and even boost, its "trustworthy and reliable status" to which all sides in the GCC disputes could recourse as a "neutral and unprejudiced great power."[3]

In fact, the Chinese orientation toward the crises in the GCC had a lot to do with its increasingly growing interests in the

---

Literature was Launched at Tehran University], *University of Tehran*, December 19, 2015.
1 Christopher A. Ford, *The Mind of Empire: China's History and Modern Foreign Relations* (Lexington, KY: The University Press of Kentucky, 2010), p. 190.
2 "How the Gulf Row is Blocking China's New Silk Road," *South China Morning Post*, June 5, 2017.
3 "Full Text of China's Arab Policy Paper," *Xinhua*, January 13, 2016; and "Xi of Arabia," *Project Syndicate*, January 29, 2016.

wealthy Arab body. The existing stakes were enough high, and the prospect of China's connections to the GCC seemed to be just bright.[1] In less than a decade, the Chinese–GCC commercial interactions had doubled from $57 billion in 2007 to $114 billion in 2016. As the largest supplier of China's energy needs and the biggest destination for its exports in the Middle East, the GCC had certainly a special place in the OBOR calculations for the region. That is no coincidence why the Chinese officials wanted prudently to take into account the member states of the GCC while carving out different routes and projects of the modern Silk Road in the Middle East region, no matter if this was not quite identical to its historical occurrence in ancient times. Moreover, the GCC's major player, Saudi Arabia, soon came out with policies which could greatly contribute to the successful development of the OBOR program in the region.[2]

In the GCC, therefore, a new strategy on the part of Saudi Arabia (i.e., Vision 2030) showed a lot of potential for the materialization of the OBOR projects in the Middle East.[3] The point of the Saudi plan was to move the energy-rich kingdom away from over-dependency on crude oil revenues by developing non-oil sectors to play a larger role in its national economy. This ambitious Saudi policy required enormous investment in infrastructure projects. By applauding Saudi Arabia's new strategy and accentuating their own experiences during the era of "reform and opening up" (*gaige kaifang*), the Chinese were positioning themselves for a role in its implementation.[4] Xi Jinping embarked upon an official visit to Riyadh in January 2016, dur-

1 John Calabrese, "China and the Persian Gulf: Energy and Security," *Middle East Journal*, Vol. 52, No. 3 (Summer 1998), pp. 351–366.
2 "China and Saudi Arabia Solidify Strategic Partnership amid Looming Risks," *The Jamestown Foundation*, March 2, 2017; and "China and Saudi Arabia to Team up on US$20 Billion Investment Fund," *South China Morning Post*, August 24, 2017.
3 "Shate zhuanxing yu zhongguo de zhongdong lichang" [Saudi Transformation and the Chinese Middle East Position], *Pengpai Xinwen*, December 12, 2017.
4 Daniel A. Bell, *The China Model: Political Meritocracy and the Limits of Democracy* (Princeton, NJ: Princeton University Press, 2015), p. 165.

ing which he presented the OBOR plans and their relevance to the new Saudi strategy.[1]

Xi Jinping was the first of China's top leaders to visit Saudi Arabia in seven years, signifying the latter's growing importance to China and especially to the OBOR. Since 2009, China has surpassed the United States as the top exporter to Saudi Arabia, forcing the Arab country to gradually beef up its "looking-East" policies. Now the Asian triangle of China, Japan, and India purchases roughly 40 percent of the Saudi crude oil, while less than 20 percent is bought by the Americans.[2]

More important, the Saudis — the *de facto* leader of the GCC and the Arab League, and the only Arab country attending the annual summit of the G20 — are the largest trading partner of China in the Middle East. Official diplomatic relations between China and Saudi Arabia go back less than three decades,[3] but a confluence of pivotal interests has encouraged the Sino–Saudi officials to swiftly develop their ties into a so-called "comprehensive strategic partnership," despite Riyadh's ties with the West, the United States.[4]

The United Arab Emirates emerged as China's second most important partner in the GCC. The tiny Arab state is now hosting more than 300,000 Chinese nationals as well as more than 4,000 Chinese companies and trade agencies. The UAE, and particularly its "entrepôt city" of Dubai, is currently playing a key role in China's commercial interactions with the entire Middle East and some other parts of the world. Around 60 percent of

1 "Zhongguo yu shate alabo guanxi dashiji" [Milestones in Sino–Saudi Arabian Relationship], *Xinhua*, January 19, 2016; and "Shate ruhe kan zhongguo" [How Does Saudi Arabia See China?], *Xinhua*, August 30, 2016.

2 "Is Saudi Arabia Heading East?" *Arab News*, February 12, 2014; "Gulf Nations Focus on More Investments in East Asia," *Gulf News*, November 2014; and "Zhongguo shihua zai shate sheli zhongdong yanfa zhongxin" [Sinopec Sets up a Mideast R&D Center in Saudi Arabia], *Xinhua*, January 21, 2016.

3 The two countries established their official diplomatic relations on July 21, 1990.

4 Richard L. Russell, *Weapons Proliferation and War in the Greater Middle East: Strategic Contest* (Abingdon and New York: Routledge, 2005), p. 120; "Meiguo de laopengyou shate weihe kaolong zhongguo?" [Why American Old Friend Saudi Arabia Moves Closer to China?], *Xinlang*, January 22, 2016; and "China to Build Drone Plant in Saudi Arabia," *The Times*, March 28, 2017.

the Chinese total exports to the UAE are re-exported, distorting the economic data on Chinese–UAE business.[1] This problem has a negative impact on statistics for China–Iran commercial connections and some others, as well.[2] As a case in point, Dubai has been a major source of smuggling and informal imports into Iran in recent times, making it difficult to arrive at any authentic and reliable method to measure the real value of trade in the region.[3]

Iraq: The calamity's silver lining

In the aftermath of the Iraq War, when the smoldering embers were taking a great toll on the country and a big part of its tattered territory had become a seedbed of extremism and terrorism, many in the West were still censuring China for its apathetic and non-interventionist approach to the whole crisis. They seem to have expected the Chinese to assume more responsibility through spending cash and sending troops.[4] China was destined to benefit in post-crisis Iraq, and its overall interests there were eventually going to surpass those of the major Western stakeholders (which had played a pivotal role in paving the ground for China to make milestones there).[5] On the surface and

1 "UAE's Increasing Role in China's Security Calculus," *Asia Times*, March 29, 2017; and "China, UAE Vow to Boost Strategic Partnership," *Xinhua*, May 1, 2018.

2 In 2016, for instance, some 60 percent of all imports into Iran were from five countries, including China, the United Arab Emirates, South Korea, Turkey, and Germany. As the second biggest exporter, the UAE astonishingly made up around 15 percent of Iran's imports then, though it is really hard to find in the Iranian markets any brand from the tiny Arab sheikhdom as compared to an omnipresence of manufactured products and business brands from the other top four exporters to the Persian Gulf country. "60% of Iranian Imports from 5 Countries," *Financial Tribune*, February 21, 2017.

3 "Cars Shipped through Southern Iran Up 85%," *Financial Tribune*, February 9, 2017; "70 ta 90 darsad kalay ghachagh az mabadi rasmi vared mishavad" [70 to 90 Percent of Smuggled Goods Enter through Formal Channels], *Kayhan*, December 14, 2017, pp. 1, 2; and "6000 Porsche va Maserati ra shabaneh vared kardand!" [They Brought in 6000 Porsche and Maserati Overnight!], *Nesfejahan*, May 12, 2018, pp. 1, 2.

4 "Zhongguo 'san bu' biaotai nuanle zhongdong xinwo" [China's 'Three Noes' Captures Middle Eastern Hearts], *Xinhua*, January 29, 2016.

5 Robert D. Kaplan, *The Return of Marco Polo's World: War, Strategy, and American Interests in the Twenty-first Century* (New York: Random House Publishing Group, 2018); and Gary R. Hess, *Presidential Decisions for War: Korea, Vietnam, and the Persian Gulf* (Baltimore, MD: The Johns Hopkins University Press, 2001), pp. 121–122.

as far as the PR issues were concerned, the Chinese were quick to rebut Western claims and rumors about their obligations and potential gains in Iraq.[1] In the Chinese view, the Iraqi mess had been created by the West, the United States in particular, and China had now been used as a lightning rod of sorts to redirect international criticism away from the real culprits.[2]

Behind the scenes, however, the Chinese had quietly carved out their own path in Iraq. To secure better deals in different areas in the long run, China threw its capital and technology into Iraq's dilapidated oil industry. With a proven oil reserve of roughly 115 billion barrels, post-war Iraq was to emerge as the third biggest in the world after Saudi Arabia and Iran, respectively. This means Iraq could be a good partner for a major energy consumer like China, helping Beijing to reduce its perilous oil dependency on a limited number of suppliers.[3] Since more investment in this strategic field could better secure Chinese energy requirements for the long haul, China ultimately became the largest international investor in Iraq's oil industry. This policy paid off within a short time, as the Middle East country became a major oil supplier to China; around half of its crude was shipped to China.[4]

The Chinese, moreover, participated in reconstruction plans in Iraq by investing in its non-energy infrastructure projects.[5] The battered and divided country required a great deal of repairing and rebuilding in order to be able to climb out of the gutter. China under Xi Jinping was particularly interested in connecting some of its OBOR initiatives in the Middle East to the reconstruction programs of Iraq as "an important country along

---

1 Regardless of what Beijing pretended, the Iraq War created for the Chinese a coveted "period of strategic opportunity" at the cost of the Americans who squandered their human and financial resources over the course of that military conflict.
2 Bruce Jones and David Steven, *The Risk Pivot: Great Powers, International Security, and the Energy Revolution* (Washington, D.C.: Brookings Institute Press, 2015), pp. 131–132, 135.
3 Marc J. O'Reilly, *Unexceptional: America's Empire in the Persian Gulf, 1941–2007* (Lanham, MD: Lexington Books, 2008), p. 291.
4 Nathan and Scobell, *China's Search for Security*, pp. 172–173.
5 "Yilake zongli maliji huijian zhongguo zhongdong wenti teshi we sike" [Iraqi Prime Minister Maliki Meets Chinese Special Envoy to the Middle East, Wu Sike], *Huanqiu*, July 8, 2014; and "China is Largest Foreign Investor in Middle East," *Middle East Monitor*, July 24, 2017.

the ancient Silk Road." China's willingness to play a critical role in both energy and non-energy sectors of Iraq, therefore, made of Beijing a major politico-economic partner for Baghdad.[1] As confirmed by some top leaders of the new Iraq, a steadily developing partnership between Iraq and China had a lot to do with this heavy investment. Iraq could also serve Chinese interests in other ways. Because of its growing oil revenues and consumer markets, Iraq had good potential to become a profitable destination for China's manufactured products and a promising customer for its military equipment.[2]

Meanwhile, the autonomous region of Kurdistan surfaced as a new practicing ground for the Chinese heavy lifting in Iraq in the post-war period. The Kurdish region was alluring for certain advantages as compared to the rest of Iraq. It was far safer and better prepared for serious works in building and reconstruction. And while the rest of Iraq was in the throes of bloody political altercations and sectarian violence, the Kurds were rather unanimously and assuredly planning their own separate programs for economic development and international engagement. They were seeking in earnest foreign partners awash with credibility and cash to implement their projects.[3] The Chinese were intrigued by such appealing circumstances and thereby began their actual involvement in the Kurdish region through investment in its infrastructure and development projects. In return, the Kurds could now offer to sell a considerable amount of crude oil to China, even if indirectly and through a third party, providing yet another insurance policy for Chinese energy security.[4]

But China's serious engagement in Kurdistan could sooner or late pose a number of critical challenges for Beijing. The growing interests of China in the Kurdish region, even when justified under the OBOR initiative, were to make it hard for the Chinese

---

1 "Zhongguo zai zhongdong faui geng dazuoyong" [China Plays Bigger Role in the Middle East], *Beijing Zhoubao* (Beijing Review), February 17, 2014.
2 "'Zhongguo mingpian' shanyao zhongdong" ['Chinese Business Car' Shines in the Middle East], *Huizhou Ribao*, August 7, 2017.
3 "Waimei cheng yilake kuerderen yu xiang zhongguo shou shiyou jiage gengdi" [Foreign Media Says Iraqi Kurds Want to Sell Oil to China Cheaper], *Xinlang*, September 19, 2014.
4 "Zhongguo zai yilakede liyi" [Chinese Interests in Iraq], *Zhongguo Ribao* (China Daily), June 26, 2014.

to strike a balance between Erbil (the capital of Kurdistan) and Baghdad which have long been in loggerheads over political and economic issues.[1] Such conflict of interests could become worse once the Kurds broke their half-hearted connections to Baghdad by declaring sovereignty, totally independent from any Iraqi interference.[2] Any bold public endorsement by China of such a perilous move could boomerang on the Chinese in different forms. Apart from causing serious rifts in Beijing's relationship with Baghdad and other important political capitals in the Middle East, the Chinese support for an independent Kurdish state would also supply grist to the mills of its own restive regions and disgruntled minorities.

Turkey: A perplexing yet tamed partner

The early phase of Xi Jinping's presidency was a rather tense period in China's relationship with Turkey. The crux of the problem was the alleged support for the Chinese Uighur (Uyghurs) Muslims by the Turkish government, though the claim of sympathy for the Chinese minority harkened back to a long time ago. Turkey was also accused of having facilitated the ground for the recruitment of the Uighurs by the Islamic State (IS or ISIL).[3] In addition to providing a safe haven for many politically-active Uighurs on its soil, Turkey was censured by the Chinese government for issuing a Turkish visa to some Uighur militants through an Asia-based Turkish diplomatic mission in order to smooth the way for their transfer to the battle fronts in the Middle East.[4] Diplomatic tensions soon permeated the Turkish as well as Chinese societies, stirring up a wave of anti-China dem-

---

1 "Tang Zhichao: Zhongguo xu zhimian kuerderen wenti" [Tang Zhichao: China Must Face the Kurdish Issue], *Xinlang*, September 2, 2014.

2 "Yilake zongli: Yilake qidaiyu zhongguo jinyibu tazhan shuangbian guanxi" [Iraqi Prime Minister: Iraq Wants Expanding Bilateral Relationship with China], *Xinhua*, December 21, 2015.

3 "China Rebukes Turkey for Offer to Shelter Uighur Refugees," *Reuters*, November 28, 2014; and "Why Does Nobody Want to Play with Turkey?" *Gatestone Institute*, December 26, 2014.

4 "Uyghurs Hail Turkey's Support for Xinjiang's Muslims," *Daily Sabah*, August 6, 2014; and "Turkish Civil Society against Brutality in 'East Turkestan'," *Hurriyet Daily News*, August 20, 2014.

onstrations in some Turkish cities during which a number of Chinese citizens and properties were targeted by angry crowds.[1] The Chinese and Turkish governments could, however, manage their politico-diplomatic frictions since the two parties had to eventually budge for the sake of their long-term interests. As a sign of substantial improvement in the Chinese–Turkish relationship, a naval vessel from China visited Turkey for a third time in May 2015, making it easier for the two countries to oil the wheels of their often delicate military cooperation.[2] Besides such low-profile and less contentious areas of military exchanges, moreover, there were some reports about an imminent arms deal between Ankara and Beijing, involving the controversial sale of a Chinese missile system to Turkey.[3] Although the Turkish government later had to forgo this problematic agreement, mostly because of Western pressures, the Chinese government under Xi was making significant progress in mending fences with the Turks. In fact, China was even toying with the idea of accepting Turkey as a full member of the Shanghai Cooperation Organization (SCO).[4]

It all boils down to the necessity of mutual cooperation that obliged the Turkish and Chinese governments to overcome their main differences. Under the Justice and Development Party, Turkey has fundamentally tilted toward its Islamic and Middle Eastern roots by distancing considerably from the West since 2002. As a corollary to such a major shift in Turkey's foreign and security priorities, Ankara's attitudes and approach to some significant regional and international issues has come to resemble those favored by non-Western great powers such as Russia and

---

1 During one demonstrations, the Turks had beaten some South Koreans citizens who had been misunderstood for the Chinese nationals. "Turks Protesting against China Attack Koreans 'By Mistake'," *France 24*, July 4, 2015; and "Turkish Nationalists Protesting China Attack Korean Tourists in Istanbul," *Hurriyet Daily News*, July 4, 2015.

2 Part of such sensitivity stems from Turkey's membership in the U.S.-led North Atlantic Treaty Organization (NATO).

3 "Zhongguo junjian fangwen tuerqi" [Chinese Warships Visit Turkey], *Xinhua*, May 24, 2015.

4 "Fed up with EU, Erdogan Says Turkey Could Join Shanghai Bloc," *Reuters*, November 20, 2016; and "China Ready to Discuss Turkey's Membership into Shanghai Pact, Says Ambassador," *Daily Sabah*, May 12, 2017.

China.[1] In addition to such decisive strategic and political motivations, economic requirements played an important role in pushing the Turks to get closer to the Chinese.[2]

Beijing was equally compelled to forge better ties with Turkey in spite of its serious grievances with regard to the Uighur issue. In line with the recent developments in Turkey's grand strategy, the Chinese government had a good rationale to come into terms with the Turks simply because Beijing shared some critical parts of those views and policies toward the outside world.[3]

On top of that, China's own policies and strategies toward the Middle East, especially Xi's OBOR initiative, were instrumental in China's rather quiet rapprochement with Turkey. Because of its critically important geographical location and territorial measurement, there was absolutely no way for the Chinese to leave out Turkey from their OBOR projects.[4] Regardless of its historical legacy on the old Silk Road, Turkey was actually thought to be the second most important station, after Iran, on China's ground Belt and Road project. The location of Turkey was particularly significant in serving as a land-bridge of sorts in order to conveniently connect the two landmasses of Asia and Europe.[5] The Chinese OBOR ambitions for the European continent were obviously in trouble without giving a proper role to Turkey. The Turkish location became even more important when the Chinese needed to take into account potential contributions of the Turks to a successful implementation of some OBOR projects in the Middle East, Africa, and Central Asia.[6]

1 David L. Phillips, *An Uncertain Ally: Turkey under Erdogan's Dictatorship* (Abingdon and New York: Routledge, 2017), pp. 19–21.
2 "Is Turkey Pivoting to China?" *The Washington Institute*, October 24, 2016.
3 Steven A. Cook, *False Dawn: Protest, Democracy, and Violence in the New Middle East* (New York: Oxford University Press, 2017), p. 147.
4 "200,000 Chinese Tourists Expected to Visit Turkey in 2017," *Middle East Monitor*, September 11, 2017.
5 "'One Belt, One Road' Initiative High on Agenda during Erdogan's Visit to China," *Xinhua*, July 31, 2015.
6 "Taiwan Eyeing Turkey as Springboard to Middle East Trade," *Central News Agency* (Taiwan), July 22, 2013; "'OBOR' as a Convergence Point between China and Turkey," *China Daily*, June 2, 2017; and "'Belt and Road' Project: China's New Vision and Turkey," *Anadolu Agency*, November 15, 2017.

A last but not least motive was Turkey's demographic size and economic aspirations which could translate into huge opportunities for the Chinese companies. Facilitated by the factor of geographic location, these elements had already contributed greatly to China's Asian rivals, Japan and South Korea in particular, in promoting and distributing their manufactured products in the country as well as in the neighboring regions. Various new circumstances indicated that the Chinese would now outstrip the performance of their Asian competitors in Turkey if Beijing could develop better politico-diplomatic connections to the Turkish government in Ankara. The latest customs data and economic statistics show that China had positioned itself as Turkey's top imports partner, while the East Asian country was not seen even among Ankara's top four exports partners (i.e., Germany, Britain, the United States, and Iraq, respectively).[1] By taking advantage of the country's location and conducive economic state of affairs, therefore, the Xi-led Chinese ultimately managed to tip the scales in Turkey.

Excelsior with Israel: Bypassing the West?

Under Xi Jinping, China and Israel took their bilateral relationship to new heights. There happened to be a flurry of high level politico-diplomatic as well as some other critical aspects of two-way interactions between the Chinese and Israelis.[2] The two countries had established their official diplomatic ties in January 1992, though the Jewish state had offered to recognize the People's Republic of China (PRC) more than four decades earlier.[3] For a formal relationship of some two and half decades old, and given a detached and often obstreperous approach of the Maoist China toward the Jewish state back in the days when they did not have any official contacts, therefore, the new developments of ties between Beijing and Tel Aviv epitomized by frequent meetings of their leaders surprised even some top

---

1 "Turkey's Exports, Imports up in First Nine Months of 2017, Trade Deficit Hits $53.8 Billion," *Daily Sabah*, October 31, 2017.
2 "A New Era for Israel–China Relations," *The Jerusalem Post*, January 23, 2018.
3 John K. Cooley, "China and the Palestinians," *Journal of Palestine Studies*, Vol. I, No. 2 (Winter 1972), pp. 19–34.

officials of the two countries and befuddled many other stake-holders here and there.[1] What was then so peculiar about the Sino-Israeli relations under Xi, and how could it leave the other concerned parties and interested observers open-mouthed?[2]

The anomaly was the success of China in forging critical military connections to Israel and concluding deals in armaments between the two countries. A major ground for such sensitive relationship was laid down even before Xi took the helm of the Chinese presidency. In response to a visit to Israel by the chief of staff of the People's Liberation Army (PLA) in 2011, for instance, the chief of staff of the Israeli army went to Beijing in May 2012 during which he also held talks with Xi Jinping, who was then vice president and vice chairman of the powerful Central Military Commission. Later, there were some reports from Saudi Arabia about a joint military exercise between the Chinese and Israeli navies in the Mediterranean Sea.[3] To cap it all, China and Israel were reported to have signed over the past years a number of important deals involving the sale of some Israeli weapons and defense systems to the Chinese. Given the fact that the Chinese themselves are a major producer and exporter of arms and military equipment in the world, their covert military ties with and subterranean defense connections to the Israelis ineluctably had a ripple effect on Western perspectives about this sensitive aspect of China–Israel interactions.[4]

Many of China's close partners in the Middle East were not pleased with regard to the East Asian country's growing military relationship with Israel, and the West, the United States in particular, became very worried about the depth and scope of Chi-

1 Jonathan Goldstein, ed., *China and Israel, 1948–1998: A Fifty Year Retrospective* (Westport, CT: Praeger, 1999).
2 "'Bajisitan shi zhongguo de yiselie'" ['Pakistan is China's Israel'], *Yicai*, May 24, 2013; "China Seeks Strategic Foothold in Israel," *Deutsche Welle*, March 24, 2014; and Colin Shindler, ed., *Israel and the World Powers: Diplomatic Alliances and International Relations beyond the Middle East* (London and New York: I.B. Tauris, 2014).
3 "Waimei cheng zhongguo yu yiselie jiang juxing shouci lianhe jun yan" [Foreign Media Says China and Israel to Hold First Joint Military Exercise], *Fenghuang wang*, August 17, 2012.
4 "Israel Accused of Selling US Secrets to China," *Independent*, October 12, 1993; "Selling Arms to China, or Not," *Haaretz*, December 22, 2004; and "Israel Set to End China Arms Deal Under U.S. Pressure," *The Washington Post*, June 27, 2005.

nese–Israeli military and defense connections. For a whole host of strategic as well as economic and technical reasons, the Americans simply did not wish the Israelis to give the Chinese convenient access to some of their sophisticated military technologies and scientific know-how. As a major recipient of advanced arms and military equipment from the United States for many decades, Israel could now be easily induced by the Chinese to transfer its high-level weaponry to Beijing in exchange for ready cash and lots of other perks.[1] Many in Europe were equally unhappy about such a possible eventuality. They had often scoffed at the Americans for not letting them lift the arms embargo the Western Europe had imposed against China since 1989 in the wake of the Tiananmen incident.[2] Save all strategic and technological concerns, therefore, Washington could easily lose the moral high ground when forcing Europe to forgo any lucrative arms deal with China but simultaneously looking the other way when the Israelis engaged in a similar bankable business.

Meanwhile, the Chinese–Israeli technological and scientific connections were not constrained to the military and defense fields alone. Because of Israel's small geographical size and consumer markets, an increasingly high number of Chinese companies were willing to flock to Israel to hone their innovative skills and technical know-how rather than selling their manufactured products and making huge profits. The Jewish state was thought to be a new fertile land to learn about innovation and creativity, which many Chinese enterprises desperately needed in order to boost their international competitiveness.[3] For their part, many Israeli start-ups and established businesses were also encouraged by huge opportunities they were offered by investing in

1 "How Israel Used Weapons and Technology to Become an Ally of China," *Newsweek*, May 11, 2017; "Israel's Badly Kept Secret: Selling Arms to Regimes at War," *Middle East Eye*, November 1, 2017; and "Israel's Censored Arms Deals," *The Jerusalem Post*, November 18, 2017.

2 Bill Gertz, *The China Threat: How the People's Republic Targets America* (Washington, D.C.: Regnery Publishing, 2000); and Richard D. Fisher, *China's Military Modernization: Building for Regional and Global Reach* (Westport, CT: Praeger Security International, 2008), pp. 209–210.

3 "China Looks to Israel to Get Its Civil Aviation Industry off the Ground," *The Times of Israel*, December 25, 2015; "Weisheme zhongguo de touzizhe dou yiwofeng de yong xiang yiselie?" [Why Are Chinese Investors Flocking to Israel?] *Xilang*, October 23, 2016; and "Does China Not Need Israeli Technology Anymore?" *Haaretz*, February 25, 2018.

China. Nonetheless, this expanding economic relationship between China and Israel was not totally devoid of controversy. As a case in point, some reports indicated that Israel had imported thousands of Chinese laborers to build settlements in the West Bank, no matter if the Chinese government had ostensibly protested over this measure taken by the Israeli government.[1]

Beyond the realm of politico-military and economic affairs, moreover, China and Israel entered into joint activities on cultural matters. By taking advantage of all cultural avenues including media outlets and educational forums, the goal was to facilitate the ground for long-term bilateral cooperation in various areas favorable to both parties. The influential media and press in each country gave a rather favorable coverage about the other party, while the Chinese and Israeli governments launched different scholarships and student exchange programs in order to strengthen the foundation of cultural interactions between China and Israel.[2] As compared to the way the Jewish state and the communist China used to portray the other side a few decades earlier, therefore, the new chapter of cultural relationship between China and Israel, pretty similar to their growing interactions in other sensitive areas, seemed to talk volumes not only about a major shift of attitudes toward each other but an understanding with regard to the role of the other party in their broader regional and international strategies.[3]

The Syrian and IS conflicts: Steering clear of a partisan approach

The ascendency of Xi Jinping in China roughly coincided with the sensational episode of the "Arab Spring" and the ensuing surge of the "Islamic State" in a wider Middle East region.

1 "China Forbids Its Construction Workers from Building Israeli Settlements – Report," *Russia Today*, June 9, 2015; "Israel Rights Groups Attack Plan to Import 20,000 Chinese Workers," *Financial Times*, September 20, 2015; and "Israel Signs Deal to Bring Chinese Laborers, But They Won't Work in West Bank," *The Times of Israel*, April 23, 2017.
2 "China and Israel: A Perfect Match, Growing Steady," *Forbes*, February 26, 2018.
3 "Common Traits Bind Jews and Chinese," *Asia Times*, January 10, 2014; "What Jews and the Chinese Have in Common," *BBC*, February 7, 2014; and "Jewish and Chinese: Explaining a Shared Identity," *The New York Times*, September 25, 2016.

The former eventually led to a drawn-out, internecine civil war in Syria, while the latter caused tremendous suffering to Syria, and particularly Iraq. These chaotic developments were also to put to the test the Chinese in the Middle East. The East Asian power had certainly experienced troubles in the region in the past, but the circumstances were rather different this time. By and large, the genesis and nature of these crises were obscure and bewildering, making it somehow difficult to quickly come up with an appropriate policy response. More important, previous conflicts and troublesome developments had occurred when China had lesser vital interests at stake in the region.[1] By comparison, the Chinese were now heavily dependent on the region for the lifeblood of their economic and industrial activities at home, while a great deal of their own expanding huge investments and business activities throughout the Middle East were equally and unprecedentedly at risk.[2]

A big part of the world, therefore, expected from the Chinese to react expeditiously to what was happening, and work actively to win over those misfortunes befallen the Middle East. In line with their teleological prejudices, moreover, many people here and there predicted that the Chinese would undoubtedly ally steadfastly, and if necessarily militarily, with their like-minded stakeholders while dealing with what was unfolding in the region. As a case in point, China was anticipated to soon join the Russian and Iranian governments in order to push back against the coalition which was fighting the Syrian political regime led by Bashar al-Assad. It was, first and foremost, China's own previous record in the region which had instilled in the mind of many people this mindset that Beijing would ally with the countries supporting the Ba'ath regime of Syria, though the Chinese overall attitudes toward major regional and international issues were playing a part too. With regard to the IS, speculations were

---

1 Harry Harding, *China's Second Revolution: Reform after Mao* (Washington, D.C.: The Brookings Institution, 1987), p. 144.
2 "Zhongdong zai zhongdong ganshou zhongguo guoji yingxiangli" [Middle East Feels Chinese International Influence], *Xinlang*, October 23, 2017; and "Woxuan zhongdong zhongguo qudai mei e" [Mediating China in the Middle East to Replace the United States, Russia], *Zhongshi dianzi bao* (China Times), January 3, 2018.

equally in favor of China's active participation in eliminating the scourge of the Islamic State.[1]

In sharp contrast to all those expectations, however, the Chinese made only cameo appearances throughout the long period when the Middle East was in the throes of the "Arab Spring," the Syrian civil war, and the IS phenomenon. The Chinese were generally absent from the whole episodes. They strived to escape any publicity as far as any of those troubles were concerned, while their official positions were made to often sound rather vague and innocuous.[2] It sometimes took China a couple of days, if not longer, before Beijing needed to eventually react to a new development unfolding in the region.[3] Moreover, there was something strange going on in the international media and press with regard to China's unclear and unfathomable behavior. There was simply little scrutiny in the mainstream media and press about the Chinese reluctance to play a visible and meaningful role in any of those critical developments.[4] That is no coincidence why one can find few groundbreaking academic works and policy reports about the way the Chinese handled the recent Middle East crises.

Meanwhile, the Middle East troubles could still provide an opportunity for the Chinese to surreptitiously give prominence to some of their own policies and strategies. The OBOR, for instance, was promoted as a timely remedy for the Mideast countries which either had been affected or were predicted to be influenced soon or late by the so-called "Arab Spring."[5] The

---

1 Ben Simpfendorfer, "The Impact of the Arab Revolutions on China's Foreign Policy," in Brown Kerry, ed., *The EU–China Relationship, European Perspectives – A Manual For Policy Makers* (London: Imperial College Press, 2015), pp. 201–213.
2 "China Appoints First Special Envoy for Syrian Crisis," *Reuters*, March 29, 2016.
3 "Ri mei wu cheng zhongguo zaojiule ISIL" [Japanese Media Says China Bears Responsibility in ISIL Creation], *Duowei Xinwen*, September 15, 2014; and "Reckless Strike on Syria a Shameless Act," *Global Times*, April 15, 2018.
4 "Zhongdong nanmin hui yong ru zhongguo ma?" [Will Middle East Refugees Flood into China?], *Sohu*, June 27, 2017; and "Can Jordan Harmonize Chinese and American Interests in the Levant?" *The Diplomat*, May 4, 2018.
5 "A Neutral Arbiter – the China Card and the Middle East," *The Daily Star* (Lebanon), July 31, 2017.

afflicted countries in the Middle East, as some Chinese assert-
ed, were "sick," and they resembled the story of China from a
century ago when the Asian nation had likewise been dubbed
"the sick man of East Asia." As China could rejuvenate after undergoing significant political and particularly socio-economic
transformations over the past century, it was now time for those
Middle Eastern countries infected by the "Arab Spring" virus to
learn from the Chinese experiences for their own betterment.[1]
One very quick and effective solution was, therefore, taught to
be the application of those Chinese lessons primarily by taking
advantage of significant opportunities the Belt and Road initiatives could provide.[2]

In the same way, the rise of the Islamic State and the follow-
up international coalition-building to eradicate its existence
gave the Chinese government another rationale to basically beef
up its anti-terrorism policies especially in its restive regions of
Xinjiang and Tibet. Later, military and intelligence reports about
the active involvement of hundreds of Chinese Muslim nationals
in the activities of the Islamic State in the Middle East and some
other parts of the world particularly upped the ante. This was
tantamount to a serious national security matter for the Chinese government, compelling Beijing to augment its anti-terror
strategies. In spite of China's growing obsession with potential
perils of the Islamic State for its domestic security, nonetheless,
Beijing still refused to give any prominence to its anti-IS views
and policy response. Even when the Chinese gave a lip service in
condemning the IS actions or throwing political support behind
the nations which were fighting it on the battlefronts, they were
adamantly unwilling to have any military involvement in such
process.

---

1 "Exporting the Chinese model," *Project Syndicate*, January 12, 2016; and
"Zhongdong zhi ke, zhongguo chuangxin silu" [Curing Middle Eastern
Conundrum with Chinese Creative Ideas], *Xinhua*, August 16, 2017.
2 "Tian Wenlin: Zhongdong luan ju dui zhongguo jiju qishiyiyi" [Tian
Wenlin: Middle East Chaos is of Great Significance to China], *Huanqiu*
(Global Times), August 26, 2014; and "Zhongguoren zhishi zhongdong
weiji" [A Chinese Look at the Middle East Crisis], *Xinlang*, August 10,
2017.

North Africa: Getting along with a new Egypt

In comparison to the Middle East, Africa has generally ben-efited less from China's politico-economic and commercial in-teractions with the outside world. Still, the Chinese approach to various parts of the African continent has never been even-hand-ed.[1] In particular, China, like many other countries, has long considered the North African countries as an extension of its Middle East policy. The Chinese orientation toward the Middle East has, therefore, been a yardstick by which Beijing has often measured its policies vis-à-vis the countries of North Africa. As a result, a North African country's place in the Chinese approach has by and large been influenced by its politico-strategic posi-tion, latent economic opportunities, and cultural significance.[2] Based on a combination of such criteria, Egypt has long occupied a special place in China's policy as compared to other countries in North Africa, no matter if Libya under Colonel Muammar Ghaddafi offered at times to the Chinese more critical raw mate-rials such as crude oil or some lucrative business opportunities.

During the presidency of Xi Jinping, there happened to be an upswing in the politico-diplomatic and economic connections between China and Egypt. Both countries had their own reasons to embrace each other warmly. On the Egyptian side, the Arab country underwent significant socio-political turbulence in the heydays of the "Arab Spring." Political uncertainty and a lack of social cohesion took its heavy toll on economic and financial activities, pushing the country to the brink of a deep precipice. In fact, economic problems not only played a pivotal role in giv-ing rise to ferocious socio-political conflicts in Egypt, they also outlasted the political tumults the country went through dur-

---

1 For more details on the Chinese policies and activities in Africa, see: Bates Gill and James Reilly, "The Tenuous Hold of China Inc. in Africa," *The Washington Quarterly*, Vol. 30, No. 3 (Summer 2007), pp. 37–52; Daniel Large, "Beyond 'Dragon in the Bush': The Study of China–Africa Relations," *African Affairs*, Vol. 107, No. 426 (2008), pp. 45–61; and Howard W. French, *China's Second Continent: How a Million Migrants Are Building a New Empire in Africa* (New York: Alfred A. Knopf, 2014).
2 Jon B. Alterman and John W. Garver, *The Vital Triangle: China, the United States, and the Middle East* (Washington, D.C.: Center for International and Strategic Studies, 2008), pp. 37–40.

ing the "Arab Spring" phenomenon.[1] A combination of political chaos and persistent economic strife, therefore, scared the life out of many willing and well-to-do foreign investors and tourists, leaving the Egyptian society virtually at the whim of some friendly regional supporters like Saudi Arabia and the United Arab Emirates to make ends meet temporarily.

In such dire circumstances, the two leaders who emerged in Egypt in the post-Hosni Mubarak era quickly turned to China for a help in long haul. Mohammed Morsi, who replaced Mubarak in late June 2012, surprisingly opted for, in late August 2012, an official visit to China as his first non-Middle Eastern foreign destination.[2] Morsi was soon toppled from power by Abdel Fattah el-Sisi, who actually made three trips to China within 33 months. El-Sisi first visit to China took place in late 2014 when Egypt and China agreed upon forging a "comprehensive strategic partnership."[3] This was a time when the bilateral commercial interactions between the two countries had ratcheted up to around $12 billion, making of China the biggest economic partner for the Arab country.[4] El-Sisi's other two trips to the East Asian country came as a result of the initiatives taken by the Chinese under Xi, who apparently found a new Egypt under the strong leadership of el-Sisi a good chance to materialize some of China's broader policies toward the greater Middle East region.[5]

Because of its favorable geographic location, Egypt could serve China as a gateway to a broader African continent beyond the greater Middle East region. This was particularly important for the Chinese OBOR initiative toward Africa, though Egypt itself could also host a fair share of the Belt and Road projects.

1 "He Wei: Aiji yu Zhongguo de bijiao" [He Wei: Comparing Egypt and China], *Renmin*, January 22, 2015.
2 Bruce Gilley and Andrew O'Neil, "China's Rise through the Prism of Middle Powers," in Bruce Gilley and Andrew O'Neil, eds., *Middle Powers and the Rise of China* (Washington, D.C.: Georgetown University Press, 2014), pp. 1–22.
3 "Beijing Wants to Build a New Cairo," *The American Interest*, May 27, 2017.
4 "Zhongguo yu aiji weihe bici kanzhong" [Why China and Egypt Value Each Other?], *Xinhua*, January 19, 2016; and "Egypt Borrows $500m from China," *Middle East Monitor*, May 15, 2017.
5 Cook, *False Dawn*, p. 109–110.

To better achieve this objective and manage the Sino–Egyptian cooperation in other areas, the two countries signed a separate framework of agreement in September 2015 when some 1,000 Chinese companies and projects were active in the North African country.[1] Egypt was, moreover, invited to be a founding member of the China-initiated Asian Infrastructure Investment Bank (AIIB) as a multilateral development body for financing and supporting projects in different parts of the developing world. The AIIB had the potentials both to channel some of the Chinese investments in Egypt and facilitate the ground for financing the Arab country's development projects by using the money underwritten by other rich members of the bank.[2]

Meanwhile, China upped the ante after Xi paid an official visit to Egypt in January 2016 during which the Chinese and Egyptian leaders could sign deals worth $15 billion in various economic sectors, including transportation, power generation, and civil aviation. More important, Xi invited el-Sisi to attend the G20 summit as a guest in Hangzhou in September 2016. Thanks to China, this was the first time Egypt could partake at the highest level at the high-profile gathering of the G20 whose top leaders had held their annual meeting continuously since 2008.[3] In order to curry favor with a new Egypt and offer more inducement for the Middle East country's Looking-East (*xiàng dōng kàn*) orientation, Xi soon sent el-Sisi another official letter, inviting him to attend the 9th BRICS summit, again as a guest, in Xiamen in September 2017.[4] These rather unprecedented Chinese behaviors toward Egypt under Xi, therefore, signified a new understanding in Beijing about huge untapped resources of the Arab country especially in materializing the objectives of the OBOR.

1 "Aiji zongtong saixi: Huanying zhongguo dao aiji touzi" [Egyptian President el-Sisi: China Welcome to Invest in Egypt], *Xinlang*, September 2, 2015.
2 "Zhongguo de zhongdong? Beijing pi zhi zhongdong xinjianhuren" [China's Middle East? Beijing Accused of Being a New Guardian of the Middle East], *Duowei Xinwen*, January 17, 2017.
3 "Interview: Xi's G20 Invitation to Sisi Reflects Strong China–Egypt Ties: Egyptian Official," *Xinhua*, June 25, 2016; and "Egypt's Sisi Arrives in China's Hangzhou for G20 Summit," *Ahram Online*, September 3, 2016.
4 "Could Egypt Become the Next Member of the BRICS?" *Global Times*, September 14, 2017.

Conclusion

The presidency of Xi Jinping has certainly been a watershed in the contemporary history of foreign policy-making in China toward the outside world. The East Asian power's desire to achieve full normalcy in the international system *pari passu* with its recognized status and growing capabilities has inspired a new generation of the Chinese communist leaders led by Xi to take full advantage of any opportunity in every part of the globe. In particular, the Middle East turned out to be a fertile ground in which the Chinese could have more resources and propitious circumstances to put into practice their recently-carved out policy of "striving for achievement." This approach for the Chinese was to translate virtually into playing the role of a non-partisan great power by maneuvering their way through the sticky wicket and tumultuous world of Middle Eastern international relations in which a fair number of capable internal and external stakeholders were rivaling fiercely for their sedimented interests.

Certain policy behaviors of China in the Middle East seemed, however, to be inconsistent with the East Asian power's longing for recognition and respect commensurate with its growing clout and prestige. The Chinese appeared to be walking on eggshells throughout the Syrian civil war, while their formulaic approach on how to deal with the specter of the Islamic State hardly made a lasting impression on the mind of Beijing's counterparts in the club of the great powers. Moreover, successive Chinese special envoys on "the Middle East Issue" were not given enough power and publicity to contribute significantly to the limping peace negotiations which have been going on between the Israelis and Palestinians almost for some three decades. The Chinese did not equally score big for their non-partisan orientation in the Iranian–Saudi Arabian frictions. In the same way, China strived to remain an impartial onlooker when the internal rift in the GCC between the Saudi-led group of states and Qatar seriously jeopardized peace and stability in the region.

Despite all those limitations and blemishes, however, the Chinese really craved for a major powerbroker status in the Middle East but they did not wish to achieve this noble objective at a hefty cost. They were not simply in favor of engaging in a Russian-style gamesmanship and double-dealing with other more established and accomplished stakeholders in the region. Adopting such a gratuitous strategy would be tantamount to, as the Chinese put it, "drinking poison to quench a thirst" (*yin zhen zhi ke*). In fact, this is another specific trait of Chinese foreign policy in the Middle East. They have benefited greatly in recent decades without paying a corresponding price. Will the Chinese goal of earning a good name as an unprejudiced powerbroker be realized, without taking sides, standing up for certain tested beliefs and principles, championing a noble cause, risking reputation, losing face, and shedding blood? Only time will tell.

CHAPTER 2. JAPAN: EYEING A NEW ROLE IN MIDDLE EAST AFFAIRS

Among all Japanese leaders in the post-World War II era, perhaps no one other than Shinzo Abe took more practical and permeable steps to change the 1947-regime. He had strong conviction and relatively propitious opportunity to go after measures which could eventually rid his country from the shackles of the security and political constraints that the Japanese had to bear with since the late 1940s. The prime desideratum was to turn Japan into a "normal country" so that the East Asian nation could once gain function, internally and particularly externally, like any other typically sovereign and powerful nation-states in the contemporary world politics. Despite a number of pertinent plucky reforms and miscellaneous maneuvers either championed or assisted by some like-minded Japanese prime ministers in the past, nonetheless, Abe and his close cohorts were hardly convinced that their country was already back on the right course toward normalcy. It was, therefore, Abe's destiny and duty to endeavor for the achievement of that long-cherished goal by tapping into all disposable resources at home and abroad.

In pushing ahead his ambitious agenda, meanwhile, Abe realized that he needed to pay extra attention to the Japanese foreign policy in the Middle East, a region which had recently contributed greatly to the "normalization" objective pursued by a number of dedicated politicians with similar ideas and interests. As a matter of fact, no region in the world other than the Middle East had previously paved the ground for the Japanese to take some unusual measures toward materializing that relatively onerous task. Some critical developments in the Mideast region, especially the 1990–1991 Kuwaiti crisis and the Iraq War of 2003, had already provided Abe's predecessors with a unique opportunity to break taboos by pushing Japan to abruptly play a new role outside its conventional geographical borderlands.[1] Various implications of those atypical policy behaviors adopted, whether desired or not, by Tokyo then could now be regarded as a litmus test for additional actions to be taken in lockstep with Abe's belief and determination to drive Japan further into the ranks of normal powers in all respects.[2]

In addition to the foregoing crucial target, Abe had to be cognizant of Japan's sedimented interests in a wider Middle East region. As a nation of islands with little, if any, natural resources, Japan had for many decades relied on the Middle East for a great deal of its required raw materials, fossil fuels in particular. Since the East Asian country was as usual importing no less than 80 percent of its necessary crude oil from the Persian Gulf alone, the importance of the Middle East to Abe's political as well as economic policies was stark in its clarity. In spite of Japan's ongoing diversification plans in the realm of oil and gas resources, the country still needed to pin hopes on the Middle East to better safeguard its energy security in long haul.[3] Moreover, the Mideast region's lucrative and insatiable markets were equally significant to Abe's politico-economic objectives at home in a pivotal time when the rising tide of protectionism in many parts of the industrialized world was taking a heavy toll on some Japanese manufactured products and export services.

Still carrying through such principally economic objectives in the region was already becoming a rather daunting matter for the Japanese because of the arrival of new contenders and rivals

1 Satoshi Ikeuchi, *Chūtō kiki no shingen wo yomu* [Reading the Epicenter of Middle East Crisis] (Tokyo: Shinchosha, 2009), pp. 77–81.
2 "'Time for Japan to Get More Involved in the Middle East,' Says MP Taro Kono," *Al Arabiya*, September 2, 2016.
3 "Japan Expects 70% of Its LNG to Come from North America, Australia by 2020," *Nikkei Asian Review*, October 19, 2014.

such as Koreans, Chinese, and Indians. Japan could no longer secure even those economic interests in the Middle East by only relying on its traditionally low-profile policy and hands-off diplomacy in the region.[1] Japan's famous "checkbook diplomacy" had little function in this relatively affluent part of the world, while its prominence in technological know-how and innovative export products to the region was increasingly wilting under tense pressures from Tokyo's rivals hailing from the East and the West. On top of that, in an age of relatively frequent summit diplomacy between Middle Eastern leaders and many of their Asian counterparts, the Japanese were obviously in danger of risking their vital interests in the Middle East by adamantly attaching to a conventionally low-key approach favored by almost all prime ministers who served Japan before Shinzo Abe took the helm of premiership for a second time in late 2012.

The present chapter, therefore, argues that Abe's rather unorthodox and hands-on approach toward the Middle East could help Japan to simultaneously take care of its critical interests in the region in both political and economic realms. On one side, the Japanese policy responses to the 1990–1991 and 2003 developments in the Middle East had convinced Abe that he could once again take advantage of the region in order to push forward part of his security and political designs for the realization of a "normal Japan."[2] On the other side, more progress in the political front had the potential to better assure his country's non-political interests in the Middle East now that such important interests had little chance of success in long run because of changing circumstances touching upon multiple stakeholders in the region and beyond.[3] Although this study is not going to exclusively focus on Shinzo Abe's security reforms and their implications for the Japanese foreign policy in broader terms, still, a legitimate question here is to ask what were key charac-

---

1 Alan Dowty, "Japan and the Middle East: Signs of Change?" *Middle East Review of International Affairs* 4 (2000), pp. 67–76.

2 "How Abe Used the IS Hostage Crisis to Push Security Reform," *East Asia Forum*, April 7, 2015.

3 Eugene Brown, "Fire on the Other Side of the River: Japan and the Persian Gulf War," in Robert O. Freedman, ed., *The Middle East after Iraq's Invasion of Kuwait* (Gainesville, FL: University Press of Florida, 1993), pp. 137–165.

---

teristics of his security and political objectives for a new Japan, and in which ways could they really influence major elements of the East Asian country's approach toward different parts of the Middle East region?

Hands-on diplomacy: Commingling security and politico-economic objectives

The main plank of Shinzo Abe's agenda was to rid Japan of its so-called "peace constitution" by removing a number of vexing legal barriers, particularly the illustrious article nine, which had long barred the East Asian country to appear "normal" internationally and exercise power freely beyond its sovereign borders when circumstances required Tokyo to do so. Over the past decades, whenever Japan was required to partake more actively in some sensitive security affairs of the world, it had to resort to its constitutional impediments to pass the buck. Now that leaders like Shinzo Abe were gladly willing to commit Japan to such external expectations, the "pesky" constitutional obstacles had to be done away with once for all.[1] In order to better prepare the ground for such eventuality, however, Abe had to for now take on some other doable tasks such as upgrading the Japanese Self-Defense Forces (SDF) agency to a fully-functioning defense ministry, passing through the Diet two critical security reform bills (i.e., International Peace Support Bill and Peace and Security Legislation Development Bill), hiking up Japanese defense budget, relaxing arms exports to other countries, etc.[2]

Another important element in Abe's reform policies was to spruce up the Japanese nationalism and stoke up patriotic proclivities among the citizenry. This ambitious politico-cultural design essentially targeted the younger segment of the Japanese society who were solicited earnestly to play a pivotal role in the country's new drive for transformation and self-assertion by adhering to what Abe had already laid out in his famous book *Ut-*

---

1 "Ex-Prime Minister Nakasone Makes Call for Amending Constitution as He Celebrates 100th Birthday," *The Japan Times*, May 27, 2018.
2 "Japanese Soldiers Could Fight again after Security Bill Passed," *The Guardian*, September 18, 2015; and "57 Percent Disapprove of Diet Passage of Security Bills: Mainichi Poll," *Mainichi Shimbun*, September 21, 2015.

sukushii kuni he (Towards a Beautiful Country).[1] Part of the arduous task had to be ineluctably tackled domestically, but Japan's image and activities abroad could also significantly contribute to the realization of what Abe had in mind indefatigably. In his buoyant belief and upbeat view, a more confident and decisive Japan in international affairs could critically galvanize into action a more number of the younger people so that their country would simultaneously get a significant boost in both fronts.[2] Abe, therefore, capitalized greatly on diplomacy, embarking upon frequent official trips to the four corners of the earth, from North America to North Africa and from South Asia to South America.

A last but not least part in Abe's list of plans was to breathe new life into the flatlining economy of Japan by implementing some major reforms known as "Abenomics." Although "Abenomics" had a lot to do with internal ameliorations and adaptations touching upon a raft of economic and social issues, the external composition of this relatively fuzzy policy guideline was equally important. To jumpstart Japanese economic growth, "Abenomics" paid particular attention to export industries and Japanese foreign direct investment (FDI). Any satisfactory achievement in such areas was closely connected to other parts of the Japanese foreign policy in different regions in the world. Various initiatives needed to be meticulously managed in order to score a victory for Abe's foreign economic policies, particularly in a time when the conventional Japanese foreign markets had undergone tremendous pressures from new Eastern and Western rivals.

Consequently, Abe's policies all had a vital bearing in one way or another on the nature and scope of Japan's relationship with the Middle East. As a case in point, the security bills were to make it possible for the Japanese military forces to engage in minesweeping operations in the Straits of Hormuz in a possible scenario of the Strait's closure due to using undersea mines.[3] As a

---

1 Shinzo Abe, *Utsukushii kuni he* [Towards a Beautiful Country] (Tokyo: Bunshun Shinsho, 2006).
2 "Japan's Assertive New Prime Minister," *The Economist*, September 28, 2006.
3 "Could Japan Go Minesweeping in the Strait of Hormuz?" *Diplomat*, February 18, 2015; and "Five Ex-Prime Ministers Rap Abe over His Push for Security Bills," *The Japan Times*, August 13, 2015.

matter of fact, since the late 1980s Japan had been asked on multiple occasions by the United States to contribute to the American security operations in the Middle East through dispatching the Japanese SDF in a more determined and bold manner on a regular basis.[1] Abe did not wish his country to be once again ridiculed and criticized for the way the Japanese had behaved during the Kuwaiti crisis of 1990–1991 as well as during the Iraq War of 2003. Although his security reform bills might still fall short of what the Americans had long expected from Japan to do in the Middle East, the Japanese could, from now on, commit themselves to more assertive measures in the region because of lesser legal and administrative barriers the East Asian country were encountering.[2]

Still some other aspects of the Japanese foreign policy in the Middle East had to be dealt with on a case by case basis. As various players of the Middle East have long engaged Japan according to their own peculiar patterns of topsy-turvy politics and international alliances, Abe had to cautiously take into account such delicate differences while pursuing his objectives in the region. Few Japanese leaders had already scored big in the Middle East, and many of them had even faced more devastating troubles than any high-yielding achievement there.[3] Additionally, Abe took the helm of the Japanese Mideast policy at a critical time when his country came across some new daunting challenges unbeknownst to his predecessors. From the Syrian civil war to the rise of the Islamic States (IS or ISIS), these recent demanding developments were to certainly render their disturbing implications upon Japan in various forms. How did then Japan under Shinzo Abe manage all these troubles in the Middle East while striving to push forward his new security and politico-economic policies in different parts of the region?

---

1 Peter J. Woolley, *Japan's Navy: Politics and Paradox, 1971–2000* (Boulder, CO: Lynne Rienner Publishers, 2000), p. 101; and Gary Hart, *The Fourth Power: A Grand Strategy for the United States in the Twenty-First Century* (New York: Oxford University Press, 2004), p. 27.
2 "Nihon ga chūtō de dekiru koto ha nani ka" [What Does Japan Can Do in the Middle East], *Asahi Shimbun,* February 3, 2015.
3 Shirzad Azad, "Japan's Gulf Policy and Response to the Iraq War," *Middle East Review of International Affairs,* Vol. 12, No. 2 (2008), pp. 52–64.

The Gulf Cooperation Council: Getting a bead on rivals

By and large, Japan's relationship with the Arab bloc of the Gulf Cooperation Council (GCC) has long moved around the orbit of political economy. Though largely economic in nature, their relations have been greatly influenced through the political will demonstrated and the political intervention wielded by either party. Moreover, an ace in the hole is their identical affiliation with a matching pattern of international alliances which have for many decades contributed tremendously to the Japanese–GCC interactions in political, economic, and technological fields. For enjoying an overall climate of exchanges on relatively agreeable terms, their nexus of partnership has thereby encountered very few, if any, insurmountable challenges over more than three and half decades since the GCC was brought into being in March 1981.[1] Even the recent move of conveying "strategic dialogue" between the Japanese and GCC members has had a lot to do with finding new initiatives in order to broaden the scope and size of their ongoing connections in different areas.[2]

It was, therefore, convenient for Shinzo Abe to look after his politico-economic objectives among the GCC countries. Part of his strategy was to pay frequent visits to GCC states in addition to receiving in Tokyo many official delegates and dignitaries arriving from those Arab countries. In spite of the overall significance he attached to the regional bloc as a whole, still Abe paid more attention to Japan's bilateral relationship with Saudi Arabia.[3] His government particularly drew a bead on the kingdom by carefully surveying all potential opportunities which could originate from the wealthy Arab country. Abe also became the first Japanese sitting prime minister to host a Saudi leader in about 46 years when King Salman visited Japan in March 2017 as a part of his lengthy Asian tour.[4] Such rare reciprocity and high

1 Ronald Dore, "Japan in the Coming Century: Looking East or West?" in Edward R. Beauchamp, ed., *Japan's Role in International Politics since World War II* (New York and London: Garland Publishing, 1998): 23–30.
2 Christopher M. Davidson, *The Persian Gulf and Pacific Asia: From Indifference to Interdependence* (London: Hurst & Company, 2010), p. 46.
3 "Saudi–Japan Trade Relationship Represents Friendship Model," *Arab News*, June 21, 2015.
4 "Sauji kokuō, 3 tsuki rainichi e 46-nen-buri datsu sekiyu, nihon ni kyōryoku yōsei" [Saudi King's March Visit to Japan First in 46 Years,

profile exchanges between top leaders of the two countries were taking place at a propitious time when Saudi Arabia's embarkation on a so-called "2030 vision" was dovetailing neatly with some of the goals and directions laid down through the "Abenomics" agenda.[1]

Saudi Arabia's new national strategy was to eventually wean the Arab country off its dreadful dependency on oil revenues by subscribing into non-energy economic sectors as other major purveyors of filling out the state's coffers.[2] Although the oil-rich Mideast country supplies roughly one-third of the Japanese imported crude, it is highly unlikely that the Saudis' ambitious plan could pose any real danger to Tokyo's energy security in short to mid-term. This is a reason why the Abe government warmly welcomed the Saudi initiative, hoping that many businesses in Japan could take advantage from many benefits the Arab kingdom potentially offered.[3] After all, the aspiring Saudi vision required a lot of fresh investments as well as access to a slew of new equipment and technologies a good deal of which could be provided by the Japanese. If approached at the right time and convinced articulately, the formidable task of Saudi Arabia outlined through the "2030 vision" could still pour into Japan a hefty of the Saudi money in forms such as listing its oil giant, Aramco, on the Tokyo Stock Exchange.[4]

Meanwhile, Abe had to simultaneously compete with a growing number of other stakeholders and contenders all vying for the heart and capital of the GCC countries. As a matter of fact,

---

Seeking Japanese Help to Get Rid of Oil], *Nihon Keizai Shimbun*, January 26, 2017.
1 "Chūtō kinchō, nayameru nihon Iran.Sauji no baransu fushin" [Middle East Tension Troubles Japan's Iran–Saudi Balance Mindset], *Nihon Keizai Shimbun*, January 11, 2016; and "Corporate Japan to Power Saudi Economic Overhaul," *Nikkei Asian Review*, March 14, 2017.
2 Michael L. Ross, *The Oil Curse: How Petroleum Wealth Shapes the Development of Nations* (Princeton and Oxford: Princeton University Press, 2012), pp. 104.
3 "Saudi Prince Wants Japan's Help in Kicking Oil Habit," *Nikkei Asian Review*, September 9, 2016.
4 "Sauji, amerika to kankei akka de nihon kigyō ni katsuro" [Amid Deterioration of Saudi–American Relationship, Japanese Corporations Become a Means of Escape], *Nihon Keizai Shimbun*, October 14, 2016; and "Japan's Important Role in Saudi's Vision 2030," *Middle East Institute*, November 29, 2016.

Japanese businesses and products were already under mounting pressures from Western and particularly Eastern rivals. Of course, Japan could count on its advanced technologies and rather long experience to partially push back against the new challenges to its vested interests in the region, but especially the Asian competitors were increasingly narrowing down their differences with Tokyo through offering, on rather favorable terms, new products and services to their affluent partners in the GCC bloc. On top of that, almost all of the GCC states had recently embraced a new looking-East approach of sorts, providing a better ground for other well-to-do Asian countries to engage in a one-upmanship with Japan in economic and even political and cultural domains.[1] This was a key rationale behind Shinzo Abe's frequent exchanges with top politicians and delegates from the GCC countries.

The stakes were high for all Asian leaders to curry favor with their counterparts in the GCC countries. As a technologically poor yet financially rich region, the GCC remained an attractive export market for Asian manufactured products ranging from cut-priced mobile phones from China to luxury automobiles from Japan. And despite its ups and downs due to fluctuating oil prices, the region's bustling business of construction had equally proven to be a tempting taste for a flurry of Asian contractors, Koreans in particular; many of whom had been further lured into the region because of new mega projects which are going to be erected for Qatar's World Cup 2022, Dubai's Expo 2020, etc.[2] True that only a few Asian countries could effectively compete with Japan to secure a number of the lucrative deals to build nuclear power facilities coveted by some GCC states in recent years, nonetheless, almost all of them could offer equally, if not say more attractive, advantages to win over many wealthy clients from the GCC countries for a whole host of desired products and services, ranging from medical and leisure tourism in

---

1 "The Gulf States are turning to Asia in a Big Way. Here's why it Matters," *The Washington Post*, April 21, 2017.
2 "Japan, Qatar to Discuss Investment Pact, Infrastructure Cooperation," *Kyodo*, August 28, 2013; and "Korea Seeks Business Opportunities in Qatar's World Cup Preparations," *Arirang News*, March 8, 2015.

Seoul and Jeju Island to vocational and educational courses in Shanghai and Beijing.[1]

Iran: Walking a tightrope

There happened to be a sharp difference in Shinzo Abe's approach toward Iran during his first and second governments. When he took the helm of the Japanese premiership in September 2006, Abe had to largely attach to the Iran policy which his former boss and predecessor, Junichiro Koizumi, had carved out and implemented steadfastly. As a protégé and proponent of Koizumi, Abe made all but little changes in Japan's foreign policy orientation toward Iran over the course of his first government. The essence of that policy was by and large about the Iranian nuclear controversy and the pertinent cooperation with the United States about the matter.[2] Since Japan was simultaneously facing the pressing North Korean nuclear issue, Tokyo had to gradually ratchet up its anti-Iran rhetoric staying on par with Washington and Tel Aviv over the Iranian nuclear stalemate.[3] Such a peculiarity in Japan's stance toward Iran significantly harmed its previously growing ties with Tehran, resulting eventually in a number of unwelcome ramifications for the bilateral ties such as the cancellation of the lucrative oil project of Azadegan between the two countries.[4]

1 "Abe Reaches Deal with Bahrain on GCC Talks," *Kyodo*, August 25, 2013; and "Japan's Abe to Speak in Dubai on Sunday," *The National*, February 9, 2017.

2 Yomiuri Shinbun Seijibu, *Gaikō wo kenka ni shita otoko: Koizumi gaikō 2000 nichi no shinjitsu [The Man Who Made Diplomacy a Fall-out: The Truth of 2000 Days of Koizumi Diplomacy]* (Tokyo: Shinchō sha, 2006), p. 37.

3 Ministry of Defense, *Defense of Japan 2007* (Tokyo: Ministry of Defense, Annual White Paper, 2007), p. 14; "Japan Imposes New Iran Sanctions," *Wall Street Journal*, December 8, 2011; "Japan Bank Freezes Iran Accounts after Court Order," *AFP*, May 21, 2012; "Abe and Bibi Share Tough Line on Their Neighbors," *Wall Street Journal*, May 12, 2014; and "Japanese–Israel Defense Accords Cover Cyber Security Cooperation against China, North Korea and Iran," *Debkafile*, May 12, 2014.

4 Michael Penn, *Japan and the War on Terror: Military Force and Political Pressure in the US–Japanese Alliance* (London and New York: I.B. Tauris, 2014), p. 197–199; "Americans Stymie Japan–Iran Oil Deal," *Asia Times*, July 4, 2003; "Japan, Iran Sign Huge Oilfield Deal Despite US Opposition," *Mainichi Daily News*, February 19, 2004; "Bolton Downplays Disagreement over Japan–Iran Oil Deal," *The Japan Times*, February

When Abe was elected as prime minister for a second time in September 2012, however, it was no longer plausible for him to stick to the same policy toward Iran. Fortunately, the Democratic Party of Japan (DPJ) which had ruled the country since September 2009 before being railroaded out of power again by Abe's own Liberal Democratic Party (LDP) in September 2012, had relaxed in part Japan's frosty post-9/11 stance toward Tehran under the LDP. The DPJ had even succeeded to dispatch to Tehran its former leader, Yukio Hatoyama who was Japan's 60th prime minister from September 2009 to June 2010, on an ostensibly unofficial "private visit" in order to mend fences with Iran, though Tokyo was still under mounting pressures from Washington with regard to the ongoing nuclear impasse.[1] It was, therefore, a good chance for the second Abe government to tap into the DPJ's Iran legacy by taking a new course of action toward Tehran. Much to Abe's luck, another propitious window of opportunity followed soon when the moderate government of Hassan Rouhani acceded to power in Iran in August 2013.[2]

Under Rouhani, Iran engaged in a protracted process of nuclear negotiations with the 5+1 group (United States, Russia, Britain, France, China, and Germany) for over 18 months which led to the issuance of the Joint Comprehensive Plan of Action (JCPOA) according to which Tehran agreed to mothball its nuclear activities in exchange of gradual sanctions relief. Although Japan was not a part of the negotiating club, Tokyo showed signs of eagerness to lobby, both officially and unofficially, for a swift settlement of the nuclear crisis.[3] Japanese officials in different capacities reached out particularly to their American and Iranian counterparts to push them for narrowing down their dif-

20, 2004; and "Oil and Power: The Rise and Fall of the Japan–Iran Partnership in Azadegan," *Japan Focus*, December 19, 2006.
1 "Hatoyama Comes under Fire for Iran Visit, Claims Ambush," *The Japan Times*, April 12, 2012.
2 "Iran Wants Japan Back in Energy Projects," *Press TV*, August 9, 2015; "Iran Painter Awarded Japan Order of the Rising Sun," *Press TV*, November 3, 2015; and "Iranian Professor Conferred Japanese Order of Honor," *Mehr News Agency*, November 4, 2016.
3 "Iran Seeks Japan's Help in Resolving Nuclear Issue," *The Japan Times*, November 15, 2003; and "Darkhast nashyaneh zhapon az Iran: Tokyo khastar dekhalat Tehran dar majaray koreye shomali shod" [Japan's Amateurish Appeal to Iran: Tokyo Asks for Tehran's Intervention in North Korean Issue], *Aftab Yazd*, September 24, 2017, pp. 1, 15.

ferences throughout the lengthy nuclear negotiations between Iran and the sextet. Since one of the leading member of the Iranian negotiating team had already served as Tehran ambassador to Tokyo, Japan under Abe found another good chance to once again play a constructive role in mediating between Iran and the West, the United States in particular.[1]

Essentially, the icy situation in the Japanese–Iranian relations started to slowly thaw long before the nuclear negotiations were concluded. A couple of months after the inauguration of the Rouhani government, Abe was seen standing next to Rouhani in the opening ceremony of the World Economic Forum's annual meeting in Davos in January 2014. They later arranged more meetings in other occasions especially on the sidelines of the UN's summit meetings held annually in New York, while the Japanese and Iranian foreign ministers had more chances to meet several times here and there.[2] After Iran agreed to the terms of the nuclear deal based on the JCPOA document, Shinzo Abe was among the foreign leaders who disclosed his plan to visit Tehran shortly.[3] He was soon forced to first postpone and then cancel the trip apparently due to some domestic developments in the United States which led to the triumph of Donald Trump as a new American president from the Republican Party.[4] Despite such a stumbling block, Japan's overall approach toward Iran under the second Abe government was way different, and

1 "Nihon ga tayoru sauji to Iran dankō de genyu kakaku ni eikyō wa" [Japanese Stake in Saudi–Iranian Severing Relations Influences the Price of Crude Oil], *Terebi Asahi*, January 6, 2016.
2 "Abe Meets Iran Counterpart on U.N. Sidelines, Urges Tehran toward Nuclear Deal with Prospect of Japanese Investment," *Kyodo*, September 28, 2015.
3 "Abe Eyes Visiting Iran in August," *Kyodo*, April 6, 2016.
4 With an apparent mandate of mediating between the Trump administration and the regime of the Islamic Republic, Shinzo Abe eventually embarked upon a historic and relatively colorful visit to Iran in June 2019. While Abe was in Tehran talking to the top officials, two tankers carrying petrochemicals mysteriously came under suspect attacks in the Gulf of Oman near the strategic Straits of Hormuz. One of those two ships was a Japanese-operated tanker and the other one was owned by Norway, but both of them were carrying Japan-related cargo. For more details, see: "Abe Departs for Tension-easing Iran Visit," *The Mainichi*, June 12, 2019; "Shinzo Abe's Mission to Iran Ends in Flames," *The Washington Post*, June 14, 2019; and "Abe Denounces Tanker Attacks, But Stays Silent on Possible Suspects," *The Japan Times*, June 15, 2019.

this major shift had also something to do with a fresh assessment among many concerned Japanese officials with regard to an "opening Iran" under Rouhani.

A new Iran was widely predicted by many sophisticated people in Japan to be a land of opportunities in various ways.[1] Almost all of the Japanese companies which had previously been forced to forgo their market share in Iran were now very keen to return back. The erstwhile regime of international sanctions, levied on Tehran over years because of the nuclear crisis, had significantly damaged Japan's political and especially economic connections to Iran. Although the bilateral political and economic ties had never been severed, the scope and size of the Japanese presence in Iran had been considerably reduced — mainly in favor of Japan's Asian rivals, particularly the Chinese and Koreans.[2] Besides being a very lucrative investment and exports market, Iran's historical role and its strategic location were very pivotal to Japan's overall foreign policy toward the Middle East and Central Asia.[3] An "opening Iran" could indeed present a whole host of fresh opportunities to Japan in all political, economic, and cultural areas; Critical stakes which encouraged Abe to reassess Tokyo's erstwhile orientation toward Tehran vigorously and objectively.[4]

Iraq: Back to business amid new stakes

By the time the commanding heights of Japanese politics and economy moved into the hands of Shinzo Abe for a second time in September 2012, Iraq seemed to be far more organized and secure than the time Abe prematurely left office in September

1 Nathan Gonzalez, *Engaging Iran: The Rise of a Middle East Powerhouse and America's Strategic Choice* (Westport, CT: Praeger, 2007), p. 100.

2 "Abe Tries to Fill Korea's Vacuum in Middle East," *Korea Times,* February 10, 2015; "China's New Role as a Middle East Peacemaker," *The Japan Times,* February 4, 2016; and "Are Japan and China Bringing their Rivalry to the Middle East?" *Asia Times,* May 1, 2017.

3 Ōnishi Madoka, *Iran keizai wo kaibō suru* [Scrutinizing Iranian Economy] (Tokyo: JETRO, 2000), pp. 99–103; "Bank of Tokyo-Mitsubishi UFJ Fined Again by Lawsky," *The New York Times,* November 18, 2014; "Japan to Open $10bn Credit Line for Iran," *Mehr News Agency,* February 6, 2016; and "Iran's Crude Exports to Japan Doubles," *Mehr News Agency,* December 25, 2016.

4 Mark Hilton, *Restrained Trade: Cartels in Japan's Basic Materials Industries* (Ithaca and London: Cornell University Press, 1996), p. 139.

2007. Over the course of the Iraq War and the post-war insurgency, Japan had significantly capitalized on the Middle Eastern conundrum. The dispatch of the Japanese SDF to Samawah on a "humanitarian mission" in early 2004 was an aberration in the East Asian country's post-World War II history as it was the first time when Japan dispatched both contentiously and uncomfortably its military troops to a combat zone no matter if they were not going to engage in any precarious warfare operation in Iraq.[1] It was, therefore, a propitious time for a more sophisticated Abe to reap what his country has already sown by engaging in that inordinately risky and costly adventure. Of course, part of the reward was subsequently brought in through the successful passage of the security bills as well as other initiatives related to the SDF forces, and generally the Japanese military and defense systems.[2] But the Iraqi perilous project was not to be only about some political and security objectives; there was supposed to be other critical economic and commercial interests for Japan in Iraq from the word go too.

Back in the 1970s and 1980s, Tokyo used to be a major trading partner of Baghdad. The Japanese had also made significant investments in infrastructure projects in Iraq during those rather friendly periods of diplomatic interaction. Their relations soured only after Saddam's Iraq invaded Kuwait in 1990, and the ensuing state of strained ties between Tokyo and Baghdad lasted until Saddam was toppled from power by the United States in 2003.[3] Since the following chaotic period in Iraq hamstrung the Japanese to do anything significant in the realm of business in the Mideast country, it was now Abe's turn to practically take care of Japan's critical vested interests there. The Japanese were willing to give to Baghdad a number of "strategic loans" a chunk

---

1 Yamauchi Masayuki, *Sensō to gaikō: Iraku, amerika, nihon* [War and Diplomacy: Iraq, United States, Japan] (Daiamondosha, 2003), p. 262; and "Japan to Boost SDF Staff at Its Middle East Embassies," *The Japan Times*, February 4, 2015.

2 Patrick Hein, "Leadership and Nationalism: Assessing Shinzo Abe," in Jeff Kingston, ed., *Asian Nationalisms Reconsidered* (Abingdon and New York: Routledge, 2016), pp. 83–91.

3 George Ehrhardt, "Japan between the United States and the Middle East," in Jack Covarrubias and Tom Lansford, eds., *Strategic Interests in the Middle East: Opposition and Support for US Foreign Policy* (Hampshire, England and Burlington, US: Ashgate, 2007), pp. 97–108.

of which were to be invested on upgrading the dilapidated oil industry of Iraq, though Japan was also going to partially partake in the daunting yet internationally competitive task by taking advantage of its own capital and technical know-how.[1] Besides the strategic domain of energy which the Iraqis themselves lacked the wherewithal to develop and upgrade, the Japanese had long wished to play a key role in reconstruction projects of the war-torn country, but this relatively flourishing business was not to be constrained only to the Arab-speaking provinces of Iraq.[2]

In the aftermath of the Iraq War, no part of the country became safer and more up-and-coming than the autonomous region of Kurdistan which made significant strides over time to carve out its own separate nation-building agenda and modernization programs. Such potentially budding developments encouraged a few affluent countries such as Japan to gradually build up their physical presence in the quickly expanding Kurdish region. Erbil, Kurdistan's political capital, also became a rendezvous of Japanese diplomatic envoys to Baghdad who frequently held bilateral talks with top Kurdish officials in order to map out new directions in their political and economic connections. Under Abe, the Japanese paid more attention to Kurdistan, culminating in the opening of a representative office in Erbil in early 2017. Inaugurated by Kentaro Sonoiro, Vice Minister for Foreign Affairs of Japan, and the KRG Prime Minister, Nechirvan Barzani, the Japanese consulate in Erbil aimed to practically function like an embassy in promoting and securing Japan's growing political and economic clout in Kurdistan.[3]

Before the establishment of its consulate office, the Japanese had already engaged in carrying out a number of development projects in Kurdistan through the Japan International Cooperation Agency (JICA). In fact, a great deal of Japan's loans and development aids to Erbil was to be implemented by JICA in the Kurdish region. Additionally, some of Japan's grants and loans

---

1 "Abe Unveils Initiative to Boost Security in Iraq amid Arms Proliferation," *The Japan Times*, April 6, 2018.
2 "Japan Approves $100 Million Iraq Loan," *Reuters*, February 7, 2017.
3 "Iraku hokubu ni nihon ryōji jimusho" [Japanese Consular Office in Northern Iraq], *Asahi Shimbun*, January 12, 2017.

to the central government in Baghdad were required to be spent on development projects in Kurdistan. Such undertakings were by and large about agricultural and sanitation projects as well as health and educational buildings in different parts of the Kurdish region.[1] Still there were other business areas which could potentially help the Japanese to beef up their economic presence in Kurdistan. As a case in point, the consumer market was swiftly growing throughout the autonomous area, providing a ground for Japanese companies to ship their products to the Kurdish region. That is why the two-way trade between Japan and Kurdistan hiked to around $150 million by 2015.[2]

Meanwhile, the increasing pace of bilateral interactions between Japan and Kurdistan has never been about Tokyo's designs and initiatives alone. The Kurds themselves have been very keen to either initiate or develop close connections to as many as agreeing and supporting countries around the world. They have envisioned a day when they could run their own domestic and foreign affairs under an internationally-recognized sovereign state totally independent of any Iraqi interference. To reach that ultimate goal, they first had to build up their own required resources in both diplomatic and economic fronts by forging and fostering reliable and lasting connections to many other nations before jeopardizing their presently precarious situation. By acknowledging such a burgeoning desires among the Kurdish officials, therefore, Japan under Abe made more progress in ratcheting up its political, economic, and even cultural interactions with Kurdistan. In long haul, such mutually beneficial contacts will most probably grow in size and scope.[3]

Turkey: Courting a reluctant ally

By and large, Turkey became known to many Japanese people from the early decades of the Meiji era onward. Of course, the real history of interactions between the Turks and Japanese is much

---

1 "Japan to Open Representative Office in Erbil Next Year," *Rudaw*, November 16, 2015.
2 "PM Barzani Thanks Japan for Loan Support as It Opens Consulate in Erbil," *Rudaw*, January 11, 2017.
3 "Ethnic Kurds Find Haven, but No Home, in Insular Japan," *The New York Times*, August 16, 2016.

older, but the political importance of each party to other found a momentum only in final decades of the 19th century. Moreover, it took roughly another century before the two nations made serious steps to rev up their relationship in economic and cultural realms.[1] Despite the lackadaisical pace of politico-economic and cultural interactions between Ankara and Tokyo during the second half of the 20th century, Turkey remained in general the most popular Middle Eastern country among the Japanese citizens.[2] By early 21st century, more and more Japanese tourists picked up Istanbul as a rendezvous for their foreign travels, while a more number of Turkish citizens were allowed to open their kebab shops in Tokyo and some other major cities in Japan. Still the growing rate of economic and cultural relations among the Japanese and Turkish people benefited greatly from a better political climate between Tokyo and Ankara.[3]

Politically, the Japanese–Turkish relationship is inextricably interwoven with a nexus of pronounced alliances. Both Japan and Turkey have been closely associated with the United Sates in the post-World War II era, and such affinity with Washington has greatly contributed to the dynamics of Tokyo's connections to Ankara and vice versa. The two countries have also coordinated some of their bilateral and multilateral political and security policies because of their close collaboration with major European countries and the North Atlantic Treaty Organization (NATO), though Japan is not a member of NATO. In recent years, top leaders of the two nations have found another opportunity to strengthen their web of international interactions; the formation of the G20 whose tenth annual summit meeting was conveyed in Turkey's Antalya in November 2015. Moreover, Japan and Turkey have long had much better and broader connections to Israel than any other Middle Eastern country.[4] This

---

1 "Nihon to toruko 125-nen no yūjō" [125 Years of Friendship between Japan and Turkey], *Mainichi Shimbun*, December 4, 2015.
2 Renée Worringer, ed., *The Islamic Middle East and Japan: Perceptions, Aspirations, and the Birth of Intra-Asian Modernity* (Princeton, NJ: Markus Wiener, 2007).
3 "Nihon to toruko 125-nen no yūjō" [125 Years of Friendship between Japan and Turkey], *Mainichi Shimbun*, December 4, 2015.
4 "Israel Counterterrorism Mission to Visit Japan Early June," *Kyodo*, May 28, 2002.

network of conducive affiliations, therefore, provided Shinzo Abe with a good rationale to rekindle Tokyo's ties with Ankara especially during the second term of his premiership.

Economically, one of the earliest major achievements of Japan in Turkey under Abe was the signing of a long-awaited contract in May 2013 to build a nuclear power plant for the Middle Eastern nation. The lucrative $22 billion deal, which was given to a Japanese–French consortium, turned out to be the East Asian country's first successful foreign bid of such genre since the time a major earthquake and the ensuing tsunami wreaked havoc in its Fukushima No. 1 power plant on March 11, 2011.[1] The project was also so critical to Turkey's nuclear energy ambitions that the then Prime Minister and now President, Recep Tayyip Erdogan, was prompted to praise it as a very significant step that would propel his nation's relationship with Japan into a "strategic partnership."[2] After all, Turkey's success in producing more clean energy from its recently planned nuclear facilities would lessen its currently perilous dependency particularly on Russia and Iran for oil and gas, though it is unlikely if Ankara could make significant cutbacks in fossil energy imports any time soon.[3]

Beyond the nuclear energy sector, however, the Japanese strived to enhance their market penetration into Turkey. As an opening door to both the Middle East and Europe, Turkey has long been at the crosshairs of many Japanese companies in order to augment their market shares especially in a number of large consumer markets in the region. It was actually the Iran–Iraq War in the 1980s that demonstrated how Turkey's convenient location could make of it a bustling entrepôt trade for distrib-

---

1 "Japan, Turkey Ink $22 Billion Nuclear Plant Deal," *The Japan Times*, May 4, 2013; and "Japan Plans Exports of Nuclear Tech to Middle East," *Nikkei Asian Review*, April 4, 2014.
2 In spite of those rosy outlooks, however, the Japanese lead builder, Mitsubishi Heavy Industries LTD, suddenly left Turkey in the lurch by abandoning the contract in December 2018, on the excuse that it was no longer feasible to continue with the project because the costs were going to double from the initial forecast. "Japan Dropping Nuclear Plant Export to Turkey over Rising Costs," *The Asahi Shimbun*, December 6, 2018.
3 "Erdoğan Approves Turkey–Japan Nuclear Agreement," *World Nuclear News*, April 10, 2015.

uting foreign goods into the neighboring markets. To better take advantage of Turkey's place and potential in the region, the second Abe government particularly pushed for the conclusion of a bilateral free trade agreement (FTA) of sorts with Ankara. The two parties kicked off in earnest their FTA negotiations in December 2014 and could hold the fourth round of such talks in January 2016.[1] If successful, a final Japan–Turkey Economic Partnership Agreement (EPA) would include a whole host of economic activities and trade in goods, investment, intellectual property rights, government procurement, customs procedures, etc.[2]

A stumbling block in the protracted and sometimes frustrating negotiations was Turkey's queasiness about the status of its overall trade statistics with Japan. Tokyo has often enjoyed a considerable trade surplus with Ankara, making the Turks to feel very nervous about their huge trade deficit with the East Asian country. The crux of the problem was that the tightly-controlled domestic markets of Japan could at times frustrate Turkey to export more volumes of textiles, fishery, and agricultural products in order to bring down part of its trade loss vis-à-vis Japan. This was a major reason why the Turks sometimes preferred to even forsake their close ties with Japan in favor of other East Asian countries such as South Korea and China with the hope of scoring better economic deals with those Asian rivals of Japan.[3] Realizing the long-term negative implications of such a major policy shift in Ankara for Japanese businesses, therefore, the second Abe government had to ineluctably speed up its diplomatic maneuvers at different levels in order to keep Turkey in the orbit of Japan's multifaceted close partners in the Middle East for a foreseeable future.

---

1 Regardless of serious disagreements over a number of issues, Japan and Turkey are pushing for a final FTA by mid-2019.
2 "Japan, Turkey Agree to Study FTA Prospects," *Kyodo*, July 21, 2012; "Japan, Turkey Open Trade Talks in Tokyo," *The Japan Times*, December 1, 2014; and "Eight Round of the Negotiations for a Japan–Turkey Economic Partnership Agreement (EPA)," *Ministry of Foreign Affairs of Japan*, January 24, 2018.
3 "Taiwan Eyeing Russia, Turkey to Boost Exports," *Focus Taiwan*, June 14, 2014.

The Levant: Venturing into open, all-out ties

By and large, the Levant region (specifically Syria, Lebanon, Jordan, and Israel) has never been pivotal to Japan's overall Middle East policies the way the area surrounding the Persian Gulf waterway has been. As compared to the Levant, even North Africa has probably played a more crucial role for the Japanese national interests in the greater Middle East. The countries in the Levant are typically small and have not possessed either abundant natural resources or permanently tempting business opportunities to whet Japan's appetite for deeper involvement. Still the Levant has hardly been irrelevant to Japan's preoccupations in the Middle East over the past several decades.[1] Since a Levant-originated critical development (i.e., an Arab-Israeli military conflict) could sometimes engulf the entire Japanese foreign policy toward the Middle East, Tokyo has long been very cautious to strike a delicate balance in its approach to the opposing parties in the region.[2] Shinzo Abe had to keep in mind this basic principle while striving to score more points in the region.

What particularly helped the Abe government's diplomacy in the Levant region was that Japan no longer needed to be coy about its relationship with Israel. A growing volume of interactions between the Israelis and Arabs since the early 1990s had significantly alleviated Japan's anxiety about appearing close and friendly toward Tel Aviv. As a matter of fact, the political sensitivity of the issue had greatly hampered many in Japan for a couple of decades to engage their Israeli counterparts economically and culturally.[3] Unlike his predecessors, therefore, Abe could now talk of forging wider and deeper relations between Japan and Israel, encouraging more Japanese companies and businesses to carve up their plans for either entering to or ex-

---

1 Kurt W. Radtke, "Japan–Israel Relations in the Eighties," *Asian Survey*, Vol. 28, No. 5 (May 1988), pp. 526–540.

2 Louis D. Hayes, *Japan and the Security of Asia* (Lanham, MA: Lexington Books, 2001), p. 176.

3 "Abe Forced to Walk a Fine Line in Oil-rich Middle East," *The Japan Times*, January 22, 2015; and "Japan, Israel Upgrade Relations as Arab Oil Influence Wanes," *Reuters*, September 5, 2016.

---

panding their current presence in the Jewish state's markets.[1] Moreover, Abe became the first Japanese prime minister to visit Israel in about a decade, while he also could receive on multiple occasions top Israeli officials who were no longer abashed to publicly push Tokyo to reconsider part of its Middle Eastern policies in favor of the Jewish state.[2]

Regarding the Arab states of the Levant, Abe strived to demonstrate Japan's conventional neutrality toward the Israeli–Palestinian issue by holding simultaneous talks with both Israeli and Palestinian officials. Such a gesture of impartiality could provide Abe with a better opportunity to take care of Japan's long desire to play a mediating role between the Arabs and Israelis, though there were little hope in the region that the limping peace process could reach a successful conclusion any time soon.[3] Since the early 1990s, Japan had pursued on and off to engage, both officially and unofficially, in the peace process negotiations by advising the opposing parties to further narrow down their differences through dialogue and cooperation.[4] Regardless of its eventual impact, moreover, the Abe government's active involvement in this delicate area could potentially improve Japan's image in the region which had already been partially tarnished because of Tokyo's policy response toward the Iraq War.[5] But political and diplomatic channels were not the only ways for Abe to achieve Japan's objectives on this matter.

Economic means had as always remained a convenient and effective instrument of the Japanese foreign policy in that part

1 "Isuraeru no iryō gijutsu ga nerai kōreika nihon" [Israeli Medical Technology Aims at Aging Japan], *Mainichi Shimbun*, April 3, 2015; and "Isuraeru no 'hassō' to korabo shi inobēshon" [Collaboration and Innovation with Israeli 'Thought'], *Nihon Keizai Shimbun*, December 17, 2015.

2 "Japan, Israel to Boost Defense Cooperation," *The Japan Times*, May 12, 2014; "Israel Warns of N. Korea–Iran Nuclear Link," *Chosun Ilbo*, November 26, 2014; and "Abe, Netanyahu Meet in Israel, Agree on Anti-terrorism Cooperation," *Kyodo*, January 19, 2015.

3 "Are China and Japan the New Peace Process Mediators," *The Jerusalem Post*, December 27, 2017.

4 Warren S. Hunsberger, "Japan's International Role, Past, Present, and Prospective," in Warren S. Hunsberger, ed., *Japan's Quest: The Search for International Role, Recognition, and Respect* (Armonk, NY: M.E. Sharpe, 1997), pp. 206–224.

5 "Citizens Group Investigates Japan's Backing of the Iraq War," *Asahi Shimbun*, July 7, 2016.

of the Middle East. The Abe government could particularly tap into the Official Development Assistance (ODA) schemes to oil the wheels of Japan's diplomatic machine in the Levant region. The ODA plans could include a varieties of activities, ranging from the JICA-implemented infrastructure projects to scholarship for university students. Because of its special circumstances, Jordan turned out to be the largest beneficiary of the Japanese ODA in the region.[1] While the tiny Arab country had long hosted a significant number of Palestinian refugees, it now had to bear the brunt of accepting an ever increasing number of refugees and displaced people coming from the neighboring war-torn country, Syria.[2] The protracted and devastating civil war in Syria gradually took a great toll on Jordan, hollowing out a bulk of its resources. Rich countries such as Japan were urged to help out by providing either direct assistances or indirect supports through international agencies such as those affiliated with the United Nations (UN). On top of that, the emergence of the Islamic State (IS or ISIL) in the neighboring areas was to only exacerbate Jordan's calamities.[3]

In the early years of the second Abe government, the rise and expansion of the IS became a foreign policy issue for both the Middle East and Japan. Besides many perplexing questions with regard to its dubious genesis, the torrent of IS-created troubles soon traumatized the entire geopolitical and ideological dynamics of the Middle East; a growing number of countries swiftly fell victim to the spreading tentacles of the IS; some other states were accused of sponsoring the IS's financial and logistical capabilities, while more countries jumped on the bandwagon to discredit both the IS and its backers here and there. In such an obscure and uncertain environment, therefore, the Abe government had little option but to throw its support behind an in-

1 "Japan PM Due in Jordan Next Week," *The Japan Times*, January 13, 2015.

2 "East Asia to Pledge Concrete Contribution to Palestine," *The Jakarta Post*, February 28, 2014; "Abe Pledges $1.5 Billion in Middle East Aid, Balks at Opening Door to Refugees," *Kyodo*, September 30, 2015; and "Chūtō no nanmin shien susumeyo" [Let's Support Middle East Refugees], *Komei Shimbun*, December 10, 2015.

3 "Nihon no tero taisaku" [Japan's Counter-terror Measures], *Mainichi Shimbun*, January 8, 2016; and "Japan's Abe Pledges Support for Mideast Countries Battling Islamic State," *Reuters*, January 17, 2015.

ternationally and regionally-loose farrago of the IS deniers by promising publicly Japan's political and financial assistances to fight back the IS, though the East Asian country was still un-willing to engage in any form of bold military move to crash the thuggish Islamic entity.[1] Moreover, Abe came under mounting pressures both internally and externally when two Japanese hostages were ruthlessly murdered by the IS forces in January 2015, forcing Japan to double down its diplomatic and economic involvement in the battle against the scourge of the IS.[2]

North Africa: Straddling two regional policies

The four North African countries of Egypt, Libya, Morocco, and Tunisia are generally affiliated more with the Middle East than with Africa. They share a lot in common with their fellow Arab states of the Middle Eastern states, and what connects them to Africa is geographical than politico-economic or cultural. The early Japanese political envoys who were dispatched to the region in the post-War War II era swiftly became cognizant of such anomaly and peculiarity between North Africa and other parts of the greater Middle East region. This is a main reason why the Japanese foreign and economic policies toward North Africa were over time contingent upon Tokyo's overall approach toward the Middle East rather than what the Japanese carved out with regard to the African continent as a whole.[3] By the time Shinzo Abe returned to the post of premiership for a second time in late December 2012, however, certain developments had con-vinced Japanese policymakers to pay more attention to those

---

1 "Japan Says It Must Look After Its Own Before Allowing in Syrian Refugees," *The Guardian*, September 30, 2015; "Japan to Take in 150 Syrians as Exchange Students after Criticism of Harsh Refugee Policy," *The Japan Times*, May 20, 2016; and "Syrian Refugees Invited to Japan Set to Total 300 Through 2021," *Asahi Shimbun*, February 3, 2017.

2 "PM Abe's Approval Ratings Rise in Japan after Hostage Crisis," *Reuters*, February 1, 2015; and Craig Mark, *The Abe Restoration: Contemporary Japanese Politics and Reformation* (Lanham, MD: Lexington Books, 2016), pp. 119–120.

3 John Calabrese, "Japan in the Middle East," *The Pacific Review* 3 (1990), pp. 100–112.

four Arab countries of North Africa while formulating Japan's diplomatic and economic strategies toward a broader Africa.[1] One important factor was the so-called Japan's "pivot to Africa" which itself had a lot to do with a fresh, hell-for-leather quest among many Japanese companies to find new markets and investment opportunities in a wider African continent. The "pivot to Africa" policy was to be taken more serious under Abe, giving him a chance to both host and co-chair the Fifth Tokyo International Conference on African Development (TICAD V), also known as "the Japan–Africa summit," in Yokohama in June 2013, when they decided to covey such a high profile event every three years instead of every five years.[2] Abe later attended the sixth summit which was held in Nairobi, Kenya, in August 2016. Another important element was a new tide of "scramble for Africa" among Japan's Asian rivals particularly China which had increasingly boosted its physical presence and soft power throughout Africa. As the Japanese could no longer remain a bystander in the new rivalry for Africa, the Abe government had to do more for the sake of both Japan's own economic interests in the continent and its international standing.[3]

A third factor was the growing instability and the ensuing humanitarian crisis stemming partly from a number of chaotic political developments in most of the North African countries. The political turmoil and the follow-up calamities in the region had ineluctably some implications for both Japan's African and Middle Eastern policies.[4] As far as Africa was concerned, Japan had to take more cautionary measures to protect its vested interests amid volatility and uncertainty in a foreseeable future. Since the ongoing North African crisis was simultaneously affecting some other parts of Africa and southern Europe, moreover, the Japanese were expected to increasingly coordinate their poli-

1 "Japan, Egypt to Work to Bring Stability to Middle East," *Mainichi Shimbun*, October 6, 2018.
2 "Japan-Africa Summit to be Held Every 3 Years, Down from 5," *Nikkei Asian Review*, August 24, 2014.
3 "Nihon wa chūtō de sansen suru no ka" [Will Japan Compete in the Middle East], *Mainichi Shimbun*, June 6, 2016.
4 "Abe Pledges $2.5B for Middle East, as Japan Ups Nonmilitary Support," *Nikkei Asian Review*, January, 17, 2015; and "Japan to Take 150 Syrians with Eye on Efforts to Rebuild Nation," *Asahi Shimbun*, May 19, 2016.

cies within a larger framework of Tokyo's international alliance system. As a consequence, the Abe government had little doubt about working with the new political systems which acceded to power in Egypt, Libya, and Tunisia in the aftermath of the so-called "Arab Spring" transition. A main objective was to quickly adjust Japan's politico-economic interests in these countries to its broader African policies.[1]

With regard to the Middle East, there happened to be this worrisome thought among many concerned Japanese officials that the political turbulence (i.e., the "Arab Spring") which started from North Africa could soon permeate prematurely into some other critical parts of the Mideast region where a great deal of Japanese vital interests were at stake. As a case in point, an Egyptian- or Libyan-style political upheaval in the GCC countries could be truly catastrophic for Japan, jeopardizing woefully its sedimented interests there, energy security in particular. The Abe government was, therefore, quite willing to recognize the el-Sisi coup regime which acceded to power in Egypt in July 2013. Abe subsequently invited el-Sisi to Japan and agreed to help his post-coup stabilization policies by providing some loans and grants to the new Egyptian political system.[2] Moreover, the Abe government encouraged Japanese companies to increase their investments and physical presence in Egypt in addition to providing different types of grants and assistances through the public sector in order to buttress some programs on cultural interactions between Tokyo and Cairo.[3]

Still not every part of North Africa was undergoing some tumults or making the Japanese queasy about their pivotal politico-economic interests in the greater Middle East region. On the contrary, for instance, Morocco became a frequent destination for many Japanese from both the public and private sectors. The North African country even hosted the Fourth Japan–Arab Economic Forum held in Casablanca in May 2016. This politico-economic event was by and large about Japan's relationship with

1 "Libya: WFP Welcomes Japan Contribution for Emergency Food Assistance in Libya," *World Food Programme*, March 2, 2017.
2 "Ejiputo daitōryō, 28-nichi kara rainichi" [Egypt President Visits Japan from 28th], *Nihon Keizai Shimbun*, February 16, 2016.
3 "Japanese Companies to Invest in Egyptian Projects Worth $18 bln," *Ahram Online*, March 1, 2016.

a wider Arab world in various areas ranging from economic diversification to investment in infrastructure projects. Moreover, some Japanese companies were willing to invest more capital in Morocco because of its relatively low labor costs as well as its convenient proximity to Europe.[1] Tunisia also shared with Morocco some of those characteristics, but its smaller size as well as its insecurity and unpredictability for a couple of years made Moroccan cities a more popular destination for Japanese investors and tourists, propelling the Abe government to adjust the Japanese foreign policy toward the region accordingly.[2]

Conclusion

When Japan's $13 billion contribution to the Gulf crisis of 1990–1991 was somehow discredited as a "too little too late" commitment, many expected that the Japanese would henceforth reconsider thoroughly the fundamentals of their approach and policy behavior toward the Middle East. In spite of such anticipation, nonetheless, the Japanese remained largely content with their Middle Eastern orientation simply because a conventional low-profile presence in the region could better serve the vested interests of Japan. Probably the only exceptions were Japan's reappraised strategies toward Iraq, Iran, and the Israeli–Palestinian peace process. In Iraq, Japan actively participated in the regime of international sanctions against Baghdad by refusing to normalize its diplomatic and economic ties with the Saddam-led political system of the Iraqis. With regard to Iran, the Japanese preferred to endorse a European initiative of "critical dialogue" with Tehran rather than adhering wholeheartedly to what the American "dual containment" policy against the Iranians entailed.[3] In case of peace process, Japan took the opportunity to develop open and diverse relations with both the Israelis

---

1 "Morocco, Japan's Gateway for Investing in Africa," *North Africa Post*, August 31, 2016.
2 "Japan's Steelmakers Target Middle East, North Africa," *Nikkei Asian Review*, January 3, 2017.
3 "European Oil Giants Roiled as US Maps Iran Sanctions," *The Christian Science Monitor*, March 20, 1996, p. 3; and Barry Rubin, "The Persian Gulf amid Global and Regional Crises," in Barry Rubin (ed.), *Crises in the Contemporary Persian Gulf* (New York: Frank Cass Publishers, 2002), pp. 5–20.

and Arabs while trying, as much as possible, to play the role of an honest broker between the two opposing parties.

When the Iraq War broke out in March 2003, however, Japan's unconventional involvement in the Middle East reached its acme by dispatching the Japanese SDF to a conflict zone; a contentious move which was unprecedented in the post-World War II era. In the ensuing period, a number of impediments considerably hampered the wish of many in Japan to secure, in an explicit and persistent manner, their recent politically adventurous performance in the Middle East region. First, the post-war insurgency in Iraq as well as a high rate of international disapproval about starting the very bloody conflict in the first place emboldened those officials in Japan who generally favored a non-politically low-profile involvement in Middle Eastern affairs. Second, the West's ambiguous and unpredictable policy toward the Iranian nuclear controversy put the Japanese in a quandary as to how to position themselves toward all the concerned parties. Third, political uncertainty in Japan epitomized by a frequent change in the top leadership after Koizumi undermined Tokyo's resolve to assume a more active political role in the Middle East. This was particularly the case when the pro-pacifist politicians of the DPJ were in charge in Japan from September 2009 until September 2012.

The foregoing obstacles paled into insignificance markedly when Shinzo Abe returned to power in Japan for a second time in late 2012. He himself was a prominent member of the top leadership which had formulated and directed the Japanese policy over the course of the Iraq War. None of his predecessors had actually enough opportunity or conviction to take advantage of the political capital which Japan had already thrown into the Middle East since 2003. Abe was staunchly in favor of a bolder role for Japan in the Middle East, and generally on the world stage. To achieve such a long-cherished objective, he was simultaneously working to free his country from some legal domestic barriers, especially through revising the 1947-drafted peace constitution. The peculiarity of the Middle East was that it could serve both interests very well as Abe was quite eager to, for instance, tap into the latest Japanese political maneuver in the region in order to accomplish part of his intended security

reforms. Such measures could, in turn, both expand and perpet-
uate a broader Japanese engagement in the Middle East which
Abe and his like-minded politicians in Japan were long cheering
for adamantly.

CHAPTER 3. SOUTH KOREA: A RELENTLESS QUEST FOR A SECOND BOOM

For a couple of decades, South Korean top leaders were hardly used to paying steady particular attention to the Middle East. In the pressure-cooker politics of Seoul, Middle Eastern affairs were by and large the purview of the state bureaucracy through which policies and strategies were carved out and implemented subsequently. Officials with a cabinet portfolio, and on rare occasions the serving prime minister, were sporadically dispatched to the region to curry favor with this or that Middle East country over a secure supply of oil or a number of lucrative contracts for Korean contractors. During the past decade, however, the normal pattern of the Republic of Korea's (ROK) overall interactions with the Middle East has undergone dramatic changes. A major distinctive characteristic of this transformation is frequent travels to the Middle East by South Korean presidents and many other top officials of the East Asian country. They have also been heard regularly to talk about the region even when their audience is entirely Korean and the subjects they touch upon have a lot to do with broader domestic politics and social issues.[1]

---

1 Carl J. Saxer, "Democratization, Globalization and the Linkage of Domestic and Foreign Policy in South Korea," *The Pacific Review*, Vol. 26, No. 2 (2013), pp. 177–198.

Essentially, it was former conservative president, Lee Myung-bak, who tacked under the belt of his political career a record number of official visits to the Middle East, unprecedented in the history of the ROK's modern relationship with the region. As a Mideast-savvy politician and technocrat who had gleaned many practical lessons from his previous experiences in the Middle East as a Hyundai boss during the 1970s and 1980s, Lee used to often encourage his fellow citizens to go to the region in search of opportunities they could potentially find there. The commencement of Lee's presidency (February 2008–February 2013) in the ROK fortuitously coincided with a surprising hike in oil prices (to $147 per barrel at its highest) which further galvanized his government into taking action on various Mideast-related initiatives.[1] In spite of his unparalleled attention to and outstanding achievements in the Middle East, nonetheless, Lee's legacy in the region was not going to swiftly vanish into thin air once he left the office of the presidency. Stakes were now pretty high indeed and his successor, Park Geun-hye, had every reason to take the approach one step further.[2]

Although Park possessed little, if any, Mideast-related experiences and connections before taking office in early 2013, still she arranged a good number of official visits to many countries in the Middle East throughout the tenure of her rather colorful and chaotic presidency. On different occasions, Park unequivocally called on Koreans, in both public and private sectors, to look out for huge untapped opportunities in the Middle East at a time when many among the Korean youth were facing fewer desirable options to make their wishes come true.[3] There also happened to be some unprecedented developments and fresh dynamism in the ROK's relations with Middle East under the presidency of Park Geun-hye. Park was probably more entitled than many of her predecessors to either formulate new Mideast-

---

1 Shirzad Azad, "*Déjà vu* Diplomacy: South Korea's Middle East Policy under Lee Myung-bak," *Contemporary Arab Affairs*, Vol. 6, No. 4 (2013), pp. 552–566.
2 Jeffrey Robertson, *Diplomatic Style and Foreign Policy: A Case Study of South Korea* (Abingdon and New York: Routledge, 2016), pp. 157, 161.
3 "South Korea Unemployment Rate Hits Three-year High in Jobseeker Surge," *Reuters*, March 12, 2014; and "Job-hunting Koreans Should Look Overseas," *Korea Joongang Daily*, August 1, 2014.

related policies or just reconsider what her country had already implemented toward the region.[1] But what was really the fountainhead of such entitlement, and how could it give a boost to her government's Middle East approach? What was the central plank of the ROK's orientation toward the Middle East under Park, and how did her government pursue such a crucial objective in different parts of the wider Middle East region?

Pitching a second boom: Its genesis and intent

As the first female president of South Korea, Park Geun-hye's ascendancy to power was certainly new development in Korea's long history of paterfamilias politics. Many pinned their hopes on the potential that her success would eventually render significant changes to the East Asian country's political and cultural dynamics. There were also a lot of upbeat people who assumed that her government would inject new blood into the economic life of the nation by carrying out lofty promises that Park and her team had made in the run-up to the presidential elections of December 2012.[2] The catchphrase of "economic democratization," as long promised by clause 2, article 119 of the ROK constitution, particularly resonated with the Korean citizens.[3] Contrary to such typical expectations, Park's presidency (February 2013–March 2017) was a messy period during which politics often brimmed with scandals, corruption, and tragic events.[4] As the biggest casualty of those topsy-turvy circumstances, Park herself was destined to depart ignominiously.[5] Descending from hero to zero and from palace to prison, therefore, she had little chance to be credited with any important domestic achievements in political, economic, and cultural areas in the ROK.

---

1 Iain Pirie, "Korea and the Global Economic Crisis," *The Pacific Review*, Vol. 29, No. 5, (2016), pp. 671–692.
2 "An Oddly Dull Election Season," *Korea Times*, October 22, 2012.
3 "Korea's Costly War on Conglomerates," *The Wall Street Journal*, October 10, 2012; and "Park Geun-hye Puts Top Priority on Economic Democratization," *Korea IT Times*, December 21, 2012.
4 Steven A. Leibo, *East and Southeast Asia: The World Today Series 2017–2018* (Lanham, MD: Stryker-Post Publications, 2017), p. 134.
5 On April 6, 2018, Park was eventually sentenced to 24 years in prison after being found guilty of a dozen charges, including bribery, coercion, abuse of power, and the leaking of state secrets. "Former South Korea Leader Park Sentenced to 24 Years in Jail," *Bloomberg*, April 6, 2018.

In the realm of foreign policy, moreover, Park's turbulent tenure required grappling with many challenges. In particular, there happened to be a dramatic reversal in South Korea's relationship with its rising giant neighbor, the People's Republic of China (PRC), over the course of Park's presidency. She commenced her presidential position with a show of lovey-dovey affection for the ROK–PRC ties and many thought that Park's enthusiasm and verve for the Chinese language and culture carry the bilateral relationship of the two countries to a high pinnacle.[1] But the South Korean–Chinese connections dashed from delight to despair halfway through her presidency because of the installation of the Terminal High Altitude Area Defense (THAAD) on the Korean soil by the United States. The move ultimately put almost the entire Chinese society in a retaliatory mood as the Chinese government scaled back the number of tourist groups to the ROK and many Chinese citizens stopped buying Korean brands all together.[2] Although it was cast as an urgent matter of national security strategy to let the US administration install the THAAD system, the ensuing political kerfuffle and economic consequences in ROK–PRC relations badly clouded over the Park government's actual performance in foreign affairs.[3]

Meanwhile, South Korea's relationship with the Middle East region under Park was not as chaotic and troublesome as those her government had to encounter domestically and regionally. Quite to the contrary, the ROK's overall interactions with the Middle East moved in a relatively smooth and progressive pace throughout her presidency.[4] With the aim of expanding the

1 Robert G. Sutter, *The United States and Asia: Regional Dynamics and Twenty-First-Century Relations* (Lanham, MD: Rowman & Littlefield, 2015), p. 152.

2 "China Carrying on with Economic Retaliation over THAAD," *The Hankyoreh*, March 14, 2017; "More THAAD Effect as Hyundai and Kia Sales Tumble in China," *The Hankyoreh*, April 5, 2017; and "China's Anger over THAAD Missile Shield will Hit South Korea's Economic Growth, Central Bank Says," *South China Morning Post*, April 13, 2017.

3 "Park Calls for Revitalization of S. Korea's Economy," *Yonhap News Agency*, February 23, 2015; "Korea's Trade Surplus with China, U.S. Plummets," *Chosun Ilbo*, June 20, 2016; "Did US Embassy 'Support' Park's Resignation?" *Korea Times*, December 4, 2016; and "Concerns over 'Korea passing'," *Korea Times*, April 7, 2017.

4 "Park Seeks to Generate 'Second Middle East Boom'," *Korea Herald*, March 2, 2015; and "Korea, Middle East Eye Stronger Partnership,"

ROK's already growing connections to the region, she managed to take quite new steps epitomized by her official visit to Iran which was the first such move taken by a South Korean president since the two countries established their diplomatic ties in October 1962. In a nutshell, the leitmotiv of Park's Middle East policy was to repeat a "second boom" in the region by close cooperation with her fellow citizens hailing from both the public and private sectors. In addition to carving out policy measures by her government, Park herself advised South Koreans, in a number of speeches and interviews, to determinedly seek for the realization of a second boom by taking advantage of the many promising opportunities the Middle East could offer to them.

Park had many good reasons to advocate for a second boom in the Middle East. After all, the early experience of the "first boom" in the region by South Koreans had taken place under the reign of her father, Park Chung-hee, during which she was also performing as the East Asian country's de facto "First Lady" because her mother had been killed in Tokyo in 1974 during an assassination attempt against her powerful father.[1] Park Chung-hee pushed Korean companies and workers to go to the Middle East in the wake of the first oil shock of 1973, which was a huge economic and financial boon for the ROK. The first boom adventure, which lasted almost until the mid-1980s, turned the oil-producing countries of the Middle East into an Eldorado for a large number of Koreans who could make a mint especially in the field of construction industry.[2] Park Chung-hee has since been credited for his indispensable role in both promoting and facilitating the ground for the highly successful performance played by the Koreans over the course of first Mideast boom. It was, therefore, very logical for his daughter to remind Korean citizens that achieving a second boom in the Middle East could similarly function as a panacea for many chronic economic and even social problems the country was going through.[3]

Korea Herald, April 24, 2015.
1 Michael Foley, *Political Leadership: Themes, Contexts, and Critiques* (New York: Oxford University Press, 2013), p. 217.
2 Iain Pirie, "The New Korean Political Economy: Beyond the Models of Capitalism Debate," *The Pacific Review*, Vol. 25, No. 3 (2012), pp. 365–386.
3 David Hundt, "Economic Crisis in Korea and the Degraded Developmental State," *Australian Journal of International Affairs*, Vol. 68,

It is true that advocacy for a second boom was the catch-phrase of the ROK's approach toward the Middle East region under Park Geun-hye, yet this central theme was also different from what the first boom generally entailed. In the call for the iteration of another boom, the educated and skillful youth of South Korea, particularly those unemployed and redundant at home, were asked to play a major role through a tenacious application of their ability and expertise somewhere in the Middle East.[1] And unlike the first boom, which had a lot to do with the bustling business of the construction industry, the second boom was to involve a whole host of industrial and service sectors. More importantly, the materialization of a new boom under current circumstances in the Middle East ineluctably required a more proactive foreign policy by the Park-led Korean government. How did then such an objective and its prerequisite influence both the direction and final outcomes of South Korea's Middle East policy in different parts of a wider Middle East region stretching from the Gulf Cooperation Council (GCC) to North Africa?

The GCC: Gearing toward multifaceted engagement

The foundation of the ROK–GCC relationship has long been based on an attachment of both parties to a favorable international alliance system very conducive to the dynamics of their bilateral connections in various areas. At least until the GCC countries were all supposed to be "close allies" of the West and they were also speaking with a relatively single voice in their external affairs, South Koreans had little to worry about regarding the overall direction of their country's diplomatic and political association with the Arab bloc. Such international alliance was instrumental for the Park government to up the ante by courting GCC countries for an all-out, expanded partnership.[2] The

---

No. 5 (2014), pp. 499–514; and Adrian Buzo, *The Making of Modern Korea*, third edition (Abingdon and New York: Routledge, 2017), p. 250.

1 Bank of Korea, *Monthly Statistical Bulletin April 2011* (Seoul: BOK, 2011); and Nicolas Grinberg, "From Miracle to Crisis and Back: The Political Economy of South Korean Long-Term Development," *Journal of Contemporary Asia*, Vol. 44, No. 4 (2014), pp. 711–734.

2 "Korea Pursues Closer Ties with Saudi Arabia," *Korea Times*, May 19, 2016.

---

two sides signed a strategic cooperation deal in September 2014 that led them to convene the first ROK–GCC strategic dialogue one year later in September 2015.[1] By holding regular "summit diplomacy" with GCC leaders here and there, Park also personally strived to convince her Arab counterparts to facilitate the ground for the ROK's larger presence in GCC countries in different areas.[2]

With closer diplomatic and political ties came better economic opportunities for South Koreans. The year when Park commenced her presidency marked a trade turnover of more than $46 billion between the two parties, placing the GCC as the fourth largest trading partner of the ROK. Within the GCC, the United Arab Emirates (UAE) maintained its position as the second largest exports market for South Korea in the Middle East, while the whole Arab bloc remained the biggest overseas client for Korean construction companies. As a long-term lucrative market for Korean contractors, the GCC still had some new opportunities to offer.[3] The prospect of holding the World Expo 2020 in Dubai as well as the 2022 FIFA World Cup in Doha stoked fresh lobbying activities in the region by many Korean top political and economic officials in favor of the ROK's conglomerates (*chaebol*).[4] Stakes were high because Koreans had long carried out many projects throughout the GCC, and they now could not afford to lose the race to their Western and particularly Eastern rivals in this area which has been their forte for decades.[5]

Meanwhile, the Park government attempted to breathe new life into the stalled talks between the ROK and the GCC over

1 Ministry of Foreign Affairs (the Republic of Korea), *Diplomatic White Paper 2016* (Seoul: MOFA, 2016), p. 210.
2 "Pak daetongryeong, 'rapikkeu wegyo'ro che2chungdongbum deuraibeu" [President Park Embarks on Second Middle East Boom with 'Rafigh Diplomacy'], *Yonhap News Agency*, March 8, 2015.
3 "Hyundai Engineering Exceeds $80 Billion in Overseas Orders," *Chosun Ilbo*, August 5, 2011; and "Woori Makes Korea's First Deal with Islamic Bank," *Korea Times*, January 12, 2016.
4 "Samsung Chief Lee Arrested as South Korean Corruption Probe Deepens," *Reuters*, February 17, 2017.
5 "Joint Fund with Qatar: Korea, Qatar to Create Investment Fund worth US$2 Billion," *Business Korea*, November 6, 2014.

signing a free trade agreement.[1] The two sides had kicked off such negotiations in July 2008 but they had failed to reach a favorable conclusion due to some legal, financial, and technical issues.[2] The Koreans held talks with the Qataris as an intermediary over this matter but no major breakthrough happened between them. In spite of this stalemate, the ROK was successful in the area of exporting its technical know-how to the GCC states.[3] In fact, export of advanced technology and technical services to the wealthy Arab bloc now became a critical focus of the ROK government's policy measures because recent serious deliberations in the region about moving toward a potentially "post-oil era" could supply grist to the mills of Korean public and private sectors in many promising and profitable areas, ranging from health care and hospital systems to information and communication technologies.[4]

In order to spread their technical tentacles smoothly into the GCC countries, moreover, the Koreans were willing to transfer to the region even some of their highly sensitive materials and technological equipment. A case in point was building nuclear power plants for the UAE as well as Saudi Arabia, harkening back to the groundbreaking $20 billion deal[5] between South Korea's KEPCO and the UAE in December 2009 to construct the

---

1 "KITA Pushes Resumption of FTA Negotiations with Gulf Cooperation Council," *Business Korea*, March 2, 2015; and "S. Korea, Qatar to Consider Seeking FTA," *KBS World Radio*, December 14, 2015.

2 "Korea, Kuwait Agree to Diversify Business Relations," *Korea Herald*, March 2, 2015; and "Korea to Export More Halal Foods to Middle East," *Korea Times*, March 6, 2015.

3 "S. Korea in New Push to Boost Non-Middle East Crude Imports," *Reuters*, July 17, 2014; and "Korean Firms to Participate in Oman's Energy Projects," *Yonhap News Agency*, November 1, 2016.

4 "Export of Hospital System: Korean Hospital Information System First to be Exported to the Middle East," *Business Korea*, July 2, 2014; "Hanjin Energy to Sell Stake in S-Oil to Saudi Aramco for $2 Billion," *Wall Street Journal*, July 2, 2014; and "Saudi Arabia, South Korea Sign MOU on Nuclear Power," *Reuters*, March 4, 2015.

5 In order to secure that lucrative deal, however, the conservative Lee Myung-bak government allegedly signed a number of "secret defense deals" with the tiny Arab country. One part of these controversial disguised deals, for instance, requires South Korea's "automatic support of the UAE in the event of military conflict." For more details, see: "Opposition Politicizes Im's UAE Visit," *Korea Times*, December 19, 2017; "S. Korea, UAE Signed 6 Secret Deals: Lawmaker," *Korea Times*, January 8, 2018; "Ex-South Korean Defense Minister Reveals Secret Seoul

Arab country's first nuclear power station at Barakah.[1] When the ROK-built first reactor was ready, Park Geun-hye made an official trip to the UAE in May 2014 for the sake of attending the ceremony to celebrate the installation of the nuclear reactor.[2] One other critical case is South Korea's push for selling arms and military materials to the GCC countries. Of course, the ROK's history of arms exports to the Middle East dates back to the Iran–Iraq War of 1980–1988, but the East Asian country has in recent years increased its marketing activities to export more military and defense equipment to the region, though the GCC countries have shown less enthusiasm for such Korean products largely thanks to their convenient access to many more sophisticated arms suppliers in the West.

A last, but not least, area of the Park government's quest in the GCC zone was the promotion of the so-called "cultural soft power." A basic goal was to instill in the minds of Arab youth a pro-Korean sentiment so that more people would emerge as fans and enthusiasts of the East Asian country and thereby become loyal customers of its products and services. Any major achievement in this realm could undoubtedly oil the wheels of the Korean diplomatic and economic machine.[3] The trade entrepôt city of Dubai was particularly a target of South Korea's "cultural diplomacy" partly because out of some twenty-four thousand Korean residents in the Middle East roughly half of them were reported to be working and living in that city alone.[4] This was also a reason why the Park government could reach an agreement with

---

Defense Pact with UAE," *Asia Times*, January 10, 2018; and "'Korea–UAE Row to Blow up Again'," *Korea Times*, January 18, 2018.

1 "KEPCO completes $2.5b Saudi Arabian Power Plant," *Korea Herald*, May 30, 2014; "Kepco Finishes $2.5 Billion Plant in Saudi Arabia," *Korea Joongang Daily*, May 31, 2014; and "Korea, Saudi Arabia to Push for Nuclear Reactor Cooperation," *Korea Herald*, March 3, 2015.

2 Ministry of Foreign Affairs (the Republic of Korea), *Diplomatic White Paper 2015* (Seoul: MOFA, 2015), p. 188; and "Park Delivers Pep Talk to S. Korean Troops in UAE," *Yonhap News Agency*, March 6, 2015.

3 "President Park Begins Trip to Middle East," *Korea Herald*, March 1, 2015.

4 "Dubai and South Korea Sign Joint Investments Deal," *Financial Times*, August 18, 2014; "Hospital Run by S. Koreans Opens in UAE," *Yonhap News Agency*, February 18, 2015; and "Dubai to Host Korea Expo 2016," *Khaleej Times*, October 18, 2016.

the UAE over a visa-waiver program in October 2016.[1] The move had the potential to significantly increase the number of Arab tourists to South Korea, making them the "biggest spenders" as compared to travelers from other regions.[2]

Iran: Where a second boom was to spawn

With the ascendancy of Hassan Rouhani to the Iranian presidency in August 2013, tackling Iran's chronic and knotty foreign policy problems became a leitmotiv of the new government. Since Iran had suffered a major setback from the nuclear controversy under Ahmadinejad, none of the external issues facing the country mattered more than the daunting task of negotiating a peaceful resolution to the nuclear stalemate.[3] After a long, drawn-out process of intensive negotiations over some eighteen months, Iran and the 5+1 party (United States, Britain, France, Russia, China, and Germany) issued a document entitled the Joint Comprehensive Plan of Action (JCPOA) in June 2015 according to which the Persian Gulf country could get rid of the international sanctions in exchange for scaling back in its nuclear program.[4] But the JCPOA was not only about a lasting settlement to the pesky Iranian nuclear problem since the deal, seen as being a catalyst for change, had long being predicted by many impartial yet sanguine experts and observers to eventually reintegrate the marginalized country into the international system even if gradually.[5] Although the nuclear deal was of high importance for fixing some of Iran's crippling problems at home

---

1 "S. Korea, UAE Agree on Visa Waiver Program," *Yonhap News Agency*, October 22, 2016.
2 "Jejudo Woos Saudi Billionaire in Bid to Host Four Seasons," *Korea Herald*, May 17, 2016; "S. Korea Eyes Muslims for Tourism Growth," *Yonhap News Agency*, July 15, 2016; "Bahrain Buys Korea Health System," *Korea Joongang Daily*, March 8, 2017; and "Arab Tourists Biggest Spenders in Korea: Study," *Korea Times*, June 21, 2017.
3 Scott Sagan, Kenneth N. Waltz, and Richard K. Betts, "A Nuclear Iran: Promoting Stability or Courting Disaster?" *Journal of International Affairs*, Vol. 60, No. 2 (Spring 2007), pp. 135–50; and Bill Salus, *Nuclear Showdown in Iran: Revealing the Ancient Prophecy of Elam* (La Quinta, CA: Prophecy Depot Ministries, 2014).
4 "A Safer World, Thanks to the Iran Pact," *The New York Times*, January 18, 2016, p. A20.
5 "Iran: Another Problem from Hell," *Project Syndicate*, December 16, 2010; "Will Iran Nuclear Deal Unleash the 'Germany of the Middle

and abroad, it was equally critical for many foreign countries which had long had pivotal interests in the country.[1]

Most of those concerned and eager nations were actually waiting in their wings long before the nuclear deal was clinched to start their own bilateral negotiations with Iran regarding how to return to the country and its bustling markets. Still there happened to be a number of foreign stakeholders whose obsessions about a fresh business bonanza in Iran differed from the view of other nations. The ROK was one of those countries; it worried primarily about how to maintain its current enviable shares in Iran just in case the ensuing circumstances did not let it to rev up its market penetration in the Persian Gulf country.[2] After all, South Koreans, and some other Asian countries, had been among the major winners of an overarching and ruthless regime of Iran sanctions and their fortunes had aroused even the jealousy of many Western rivals.[3] Koreans were, therefore, very anxious to safeguard their pivotal interests in Iran when the Persian Gulf country was moving to confidently mend fences with the West and consequently let into the country a slew of new voracious competitors from almost every part of the world.[4]

Consequently, Park Geun-hye became the first South Korean president to pay an official visit to Iran, on May 1–4, 2016. Prior to Park's trip to Iran, no Korean top leader, not even a North Korean paramount leader, had gone to the Persian Gulf country. In fact, such a crucial event had not taken place even during the reign of her father, Park Chung-hee, when the ROK and Iran enjoyed a more propitious environment in their bilateral relations. For an uninterrupted diplomatic relationship of more

East'?" *CNN*, November 26, 2013; and "With Iran Deal, Obama Seeks 'Nixon in China' Moment," *Al Jazeera*, March 12, 2015.
1 "Iran Welcomes 145 Delegations from 48 Countries in 9 Months," *Mehr News Agency*, January 2, 2016.
2 Ministry of Foreign Affairs (the Republic of Korea), *Diplomatic White Paper 2016*, pp. 200–201.
3 "60% of Iranian Imports from 5 Countries," *Financial Tribune*, February 21, 2017; "Hyundai Engineering Wins 3.3 Bil-dollar Petchem Deal in Iran," *Dong-A Ilbo*, March 14, 2017; and "Iran Says $13b Korean Finance on the Way," *Financial Tribune*, June 17, 2017.
4 "Hanguk wegyojanggwan 14nyeonman Iran pangmun...bukhan-e mesiji?" [South Korean Foreign Minister Visits Iran after 14 Years... Messages to North Korea?], *Yonhap News TV*, November 7, 2015.

than six decades old, therefore, much importance was attached to Park's tour to Tehran.[1] Moreover, the South Korean president embarked upon her journey at a crucial time when there was really not much certainty about the prospect of Iran's ongoing yet cautious interactions with a number of influential Western countries. Whether or not the United States had already endorsed Park's Iran visit, no matter explicitly or implicitly, she most probably could not plan for such event in the absence of a tacit agreement from the Obama administration. After all, a great deal of the cold environment in the ROK's political ties with Iran had to do with Washington's policies toward Tehran during the past four decades.[2]

That is one pivotal reason why so much stuff was published and broadcasted here and there about economic and cultural aspects of her Iran trip in order to water down the political significance of the very development. The better to skillfully divert all interested international attentions from the foregoing political element, Park's trip to Tehran was dubbed largely as "economic diplomacy," "sales diplomacy," "cultural diplomacy," "Roosari diplomacy," and so on. Little, if anything at all, was said about the invisible role of the US factor in arranging and making possible a politically sensitive official trip of such genre. Although the Iranian nuclear deal had brought some crucial positive changes to Tehran's overall interactions with the outside world, still many close allies of the United States kept behaving prudently in dealing with Iran. As a case in point, the Japanese Prime Minister, Shinzo Abe, later had to put on hold his scheduled official visit to Tehran until after the American presidential elections in November 2016.[3]

Regardless of the US component adumbrated above, Park's Tehran adventure was critical for both the ROK and Iran politi-

---

1 "New Gov't Center to Support Business with Iran," *Chosun Ilbo*, January 26, 2016; and "Pak daetongryeong, Iran sales wegyo sijak" [President Park Kicks off Sales Diplomacy with Iran], *Hankook Ilbo*, May 2, 2016.
2 "South Korea's Iran," *Project Syndicate*, March 14, 2012; and "Safir koreye jenoobi dar goftegoo ba 'Ghanoon': Omidvarim ravabet be Iran be doran pish az tahrim baz gardad" [South Korean Ambassador in Conversation with 'Ghanoon': Hope to Revive Our Pre-Sanctions Relationship with Iran], *Ghanoon Daily*, May 28, 2017, p. 3.
3 "Abe Eyes Visiting Iran in August," *Kyodo News Agency*, April 6, 2016.

cally, economically, and even culturally. A key objective was to stir up enough enthusiasm and verve for a new all-out relationship between the two countries in the wake of the Iranian nuclear deal.[1] The political message of the trip was already crystal clear, while the economic weight of Park's entourage surprisingly transpired to be "the largest business delegation in the history of Korean presidential trips" to a foreign country.[2] It was estimated that the flurry of lucrative deals that were signed between the two countries during Park's visit was worth more than $37 billion, providing a better ground for Korean companies to participate in many new projects in Iran ranging from construction to energy facilities.[3] Her politico-economic mission to Iran was eventually to benefit all those 236 participating entities, involving representatives of 146 small and medium-sized companies, 38 giant corporations, and 52 bodies affiliated with business organizations, public institutions, and hospitals. Park particularly raised the ante when she dubbed Iran "a land of opportunity," and urged her fellow citizens on multiple occasions to repeat a "second Middle East boom" by taking advantage of the huge opportunities the Persian Gulf country could present.[4]

---

1 "South Korea Set to Make Oil Payment to Iran - Sources," *Reuters*, February 12, 2014; "Tehran, Seoul Promoting Banking Relation," *Tehran Times*, May 3, 2016; "'S Korea Near Deal to Sell Iran 10 Ships'," *Press TV*, December 3, 2016; and "S Korea's Oil Imports from Iran Up 8 Times," *Press TV*, January 15, 2017.

2 "Rekindling an Age-Old Friendship: Presidential Visit to Iran Helps Revive Ties that Go Back 1,500 Years," *Korea Monthly Magazine*, June 2016, p. 41; and "2nd Middle East Boom Expected: S. Korea Made Agreement for Largest-ever Economic Cooperation with Iran," *Korea Business*, July 4, 2016.

3 "Korea Focusing on Small, Midsize Businesses in Iran: Envoy," *Tasnim News Agency*, July, 24, 2017; "Iranian, S. Korean Private Sectors Ink 10 MOUs on Technology Transfer," *Tehran Times*, July 25, 2017; and "Hyundai Asserting Stronger Presence in Iran Auto Industry," *Financial Tribune*, January 16, 2018.

4 "Hozour nakhostvazir asbagh koreye jenoobi dar Hamshahri [Former South Korean Premier Visits Hamshahri], *Hamshahri*, February 29, 2016, p. 1; "Iran is Land of Opportunity: Park," *Korea Times*, May 4, 2016; and "Hyundai Seals Major Iran Shipbuilding Deals," *Iran Daily*, December 10, 2016, pp. 1, 4.

Iraq: Venturing into a new bridgehead

Under Park Geun-hye, the ROK's political, and especially economic, connections to Iraq also grew by leaps and bounds. The Koreans tried especially to pitch their own country as a role model so that the Iraqis take the nation-building struggle of the East Asian country in the aftermath of the Korean War as a blueprint for reconstructing the new Iraq.[1] Such a strategy provided the ROK with lots of fresh opportunities in Iraq in diplomatic and economic areas. In particular, South Korea drew a bead on the Middle East country's promising oil industry. Iraq's dilapidated oil industry certainly needed a lot of new investments some of which could be financed by the ROK, which was in a convenient position to do so largely thanks to its peculiar policy toward the Iraq War.[2] Moreover, South Korea gradually increased its oil imports from Iraq at the cost of other oil producers in the region, Iran and Oman in particular. This policy soon turned Iraq into the fourth, and later third, top supplier of crude oil to the ROK after Saudi Arabia, Kuwait, and the UAE, respectively.

Construction was a second area that greatly attracted the attention of South Korea. Iraq had never used to be a major purveyor of construction deals for the ROK Even in the heydays of the first Middle East boom of the 1970s and 1980s. But circumstances were significantly different now. Despite its shocking instability and ghastly domestic problems, the new Iraq gradually became a major construction market for South Korean contractors.[3] In fact, the Middle East country emerged eventually as the biggest contributor to overseas Korean builders before the Park presidency was over. Iraq had now become a major exporter of crude oil within the Organization of the Petroleum Exporting Countries (OPEC), and part of the revenues were naturally

1 Ministry of Foreign Affairs (the Republic of Korea), *Diplomatic White Paper 2016*, pp. 201–202.
2 "Korea Begins to Import Oil from U.S.," *Korea Herald*, October 31, 2014; and "Mideast Crisis: Korea Has Become More Dependent on Crude Oil from the Middle East," *Business Korea*, May 19, 2015.
3 "Korea's Hyundai Gains Lion Share of Iran's Car Imports Market," *Trend News Agency*, November 16, 2014; "Park Calls for 2nd Middle East Boom," *Korea Times*, March 19, 2015; and "'Maskan koree' dar rah ast" ['Korean Housing' Underway], *Tabnak*, October 29, 2015.

pouring into the construction business for which many Korean companies had a phenomenal forte. Lucrative offers by the central Iraqi government led to the participation of more than one hundred Korean companies with around fifteen hundred employees to carry out infrastructure projects in safer regions of Iraq.[1]

Besides construction, Iraq also became a new bustling exports market for other Korean goods and services. The Middle Eastern country has a relatively large population, and its consumer market could grow swiftly as Iraq received more oil income. Since the ROK was more interested in relatively profitable and large deals, contracts signed by the central Iraqi government could better meet some of its expectations from a new Iraq.[2] Such business deals would be even more compelling if the Koreans were to experience them for the "first time" in the region.[3] A case in point is an arms contract between Korea Aerospace Industries and the Iraqi government to sell to the latter some twenty-four units of the ROK's T-50 light fighter jets.[4] The package deal, which was signed in the first year of the Park presidency, valued more than two billion dollars, including pilot training and other supportive services for a revitalizing and modernizing Iraqi air force. The landmark arms deal was the single most lucrative military export the ROK had ever experienced.[5]

Meanwhile, the relatively more stable and quickly developing region of northern Iraq, Kurdistan, remained as a critical part of the ROK's foreign policy toward the new Iraq. In fact, the capital of the Kurdish region, Irbil, became the cynosure of South Korea after the outbreak of the Iraq War, when the East Asian country dispatched, unexpectedly, an army of some 3600 of its

---

1 "Iraqi Instability Hits Korean Companies," *Korea Times*, June 13, 2014; and "S. Korea Holds Meeting on Biz Impact from Iraq Instability," *Korea Herald*, June 15, 2014.

2 "Korean Builders Find Breakthrough Overseas," *Korea Times*, June 5, 2014; and "Companies Cast a Wary Eye on Iraq," *Korea Joongang Daily*, June 16, 2014.

3 "South Korean Refiners to Drive up Term Crude Buying from Iraq," *Reuters*, February 28, 2014.

4 "Korea to Sell 24 Units of T-50IQ to Iraq," *Arirang News*, December 13, 2013; and "Iraq Receives First Batch of South Korean T-50 Fighter Jets," *Xinhua*, March 16, 2017.

5 "Korea Exports 24 Attack Jets to Iraq," *Korea Times*, December 12, 2013.

military forces as the third largest contingent of foreign forces, right behind the United States and United Kingdom, respectively.[1] Although the Korean forces that were stationed in Kurdistan apparently were not involved in any bloody missions during the internecine conflict, their presence in the region subsequently cemented a rather close relationship, both politically and economically, between the Kurdistan Regional Government (KRG) and the ROK. Under Park, bilateral interactions between the two parties increased further, persuading the South Korean government to elevate the status of its Irbil-based liaison office to that of a consulate that functioned practically like an embassy.[2]

Long before establishing its politico-diplomatic mission in Kurdistan, however, the ROK had set up its own official economic representative in the Kurdish region. Created in 2004, the Irbil-based office of the Korean International Cooperation Agency (KOICA) was in charge of implementing and supervising Korean government-financed projects throughout the Kurdish region. The private sector of the ROK swiftly joined the business, taking on various construction projects, ranging from sewage and water irrigation systems to apartment complexes and airport runway.[3] The ace in the hole was the goodwill of many top Kurdish officials who were willing to offer a generous and growing number of lucrative deals, in both construction and consumer markets, to South Korean businesses, hoping that this engagement with the ROK and its well-to-do corporations would in turn translate into more political support for the ambitious KRG particularly at a critical time when a Korean national, Ban Ki-moon, was in charge of the United Nations.[4]

---

1 "South Korea Secures Deal to Develop Kurdistan Oil Fields," *Financial Times*, February 15, 2008.
2 "S. Korea Opens Official Diplomatic Mission in Irbil," *Yonhap News Agency*, September 17, 2016.
3 "Kurdish Foreign Relations Head Talks Investment Opportunities in Korea," *Rudaw*, August 31, 2016.
4 "Iraqi Kurds Hope to Do Business With Japan, China, South Korea," *Sputnik International*, June 4, 2016; and "South Korea to Relax Travel Restrictions to Iraq, Citing Business," *Rudaw*, May 11, 2017.

Turkey: From brotherhood to brotherly friendship

The identity of Turkey, both internationally and regionally, has long been an important factor in the Seoul–Ankara relationship. The ROK government has for decades dubbed Turkey a non-Middle Eastern state, putting it dubiously in the category of European countries. But some seismic developments in Turkey's foreign and domestic affairs during the past one and half decades have somehow put South Korea over a barrel. By distancing itself considerably from Ankara's erstwhile euphoria for Europe, the Erdogan-led Justice and Development Party has greatly shifted Turkey toward the Middle East, giving a significant boost to the country's historical and cultural affinity with the region. Moreover, the Islamic proclivities of Erdogan's political party and some other religion-related developments in the Middle East pressed the ROK government to deal with the new Turkey rather cautiously. Some South Korean top officials were now relatively reluctant to comfortably call the Turks their "brothers in blood," an expression that was previously common in many official meetings and diplomatic conversations involving high-ranking people from the two countries.[1]

In spite of Seoul's prudent approach to Ankara under Park, nonetheless, Turkey remained as usual one of the closest partners of the ROK in the Middle East. Even Erdogan's masculine politics and Park's gender identity could hardly make a serious dent in the edifice of bilateral ties between the two parties. The intimate nature of their relationship has some historical background, but its modern cause largely dates back to the Korean War of 1950–1953 during which Turkey sent some fifteen thousand soldiers to the internecine conflict to fight in favor of South Korea.[2] From the very beginning, the move was highly controversial among the Turkish population because their country was the fourth biggest supplier of soldiers among the sixteen coun-

---

1 "Turkey, Korea Blood Brothers," *Korea Times*, June 3, 2007; "Turkey — Brother Nation of Korea," *Korea Times*, November 15, 2015; and "Turkey, South Korea Celebrate 60 Years of Exemplary Diplomatic Relations," *Daily Sabah*, March 8, 2017.

2 Steven Casey, *Selling the Korean War: Propaganda, Politics, and Public Opinion in the United States, 1950–1953* (New York: Oxford University Press, 2008), pp. 29–31.

tries which entered the conflict to save the ROK. More than 720 soldiers, or some 5 percent, of the dispatched Turkish troops lost their lives over the course of the bloody war, though their sacrificed blood has since continued to play an indispensable role behind all good interactions between the two countries in various political, economic, and cultural realms.[1]

Still, the friendly dynamics of the ROK–Turkey connection were not devoid of disagreements and frictions. Troubles in their bilateral relations could occur potentially in any strategic, political, and economic field. For instance, one case was the unhappiness of Erdogan's Turkey with a bid by the ROK government's Korea Gas Corporation (KOGAS) to engage in gas exploration offshore of Greek Cyprus. Another case was the Erdogan government's suspicion about potential collusion between the Park government and the Obama administration with regard to his arch-rival, Fethullah Gulen, the founder of the Gulen movement, which was widely accused by Turkish authorities of being behind the ostensibly military coup attempt in Turkey in July 2016.[2] Of course, such incidents were temporary and could be ironed out smoothly by the officials of the two countries. But the nature of economic turnover between the ROK and Turkey often proved to be a lasting source of grievances echoed here and there especially by the Turkish media and politicians in Ankara.[3]

The crux of the problem is that Turkey has long suffered from a whopping trade deficit with South Korea. Latest statistics indicate that the ROK's exports to Turkey valued more than $6.4 billion in 2016, while the entire volume of the Turkish exports to South Korea in the same period was not worth more than $518 million, causing an astonishingly twelve-fold trade deficit in favor of Seoul. Unlike South Korea's other major trading partners in the Middle East region, Turkey does not export fossil fuel energies and its agricultural and tourism industries are often struggling to partially make up for what the country needs to

---

1 Ismail Soysal, *Soguk Savas Donemi ve Turkiye: Olaylar Kronolojisi* (1945–1975) [The Cold War Period and Turkey: Chronology of Events (1945–1975)] (Istanbul: ISIS Yayincilik, 1997), p. 179.
2 "Turkey Sends Korea 'Terror' List in Wake of Coup Bid," *Korea Times*, August 3, 2016.
3 "S. Korean FM: Turkey among Best Partners in Middle East," *Today's Zaman*, April 16, 2013.

import from the ROK every year.[1] On top of that, South Korea has long been addicted to exports, taking advantage of any technicalities and legal frameworks in its international interactions to bar more volumes of imports into its borders. In fact, the ROK has the highest rate of dependence on exports among all OECD countries (a club which does include Turkey as well), and such unhealthy economic and commercial trend is only increasing without any panacea in sight.[2]

Negotiating a free trade agreement with Turkey was a strategy for the ROK to show that it was willing to have some sort of symbiotic relationship with the Middle Eastern country. However, the signed trade policy, which came into effect in the first year of Park's presidency, concentrates heavily on the investments and service sectors involving the two nations.[3] As a corollary to that, more South Korean companies have been pushed to invest in Turkey, engaging in many new projects from building spectacular bridges to constructing sophisticated solar plants. Some of the recent construction deals in Turkey carried out by South Korean companies include the third Bosphorus Bridge, a tunnel under the Bosphorus, a coal-powered power plant, and an oil refinery. The only problem is that a growing presence of Korean corporations in Turkey as an outcome of the implemented free trade agreement has done little, if any, to hack away at a widening gap in the Turkish trade balance with the ROK, which some in Turkey call a "one-way commerce" in favor of the East Asian country.[4]

---

1 "Turkey, South Korea Collaborate on Mega Projects," *Anadolu Agency*, March 17, 2017; and "Erdogan to Visit South Korea in May for Official Talks," *Anadolu Agency*, April 25, 2018.
2 "Turkish Economy Min. to Visit South Korea to Boost Trade," *World Bulletin*, February 21, 2015; and "South Koreans to Increase Investments in Turkey," *Daily Sabah*, July 25, 2017.
3 "Turkey, South Korea Sign Major Trade Deal," *Hurriyet Daily News*, June 9, 2014.
4 "South Korean Money Pouring into Turkey," *Nikkei Asian Review*, May 23, 2017.

The Levant region: Still politically perplexed and economically untapped

For decades, the Levant region (consisting of Syria, Lebanon, Jordan, and Israel) used to be more of a political liability than an economic prize for South Korea. During the past two decades, however, the ROK government has strived to forge normal political and economic connections to the region. But the Koreans have been more successful in achieving this objective in Israel than in other states of the Levant. Under Park Geun-hye, South Korea made more attempts to increase the volume of economic and technological cooperation with the Jewish state, though the level of political and security interactions between the two countries made more progress as well.[1] Under the banner of "creative economy," a number of joint R&D projects were implemented between the ROK and Israel so that the Koreans have a better chance to learn some innovative ideas through closer association with their Israeli counterparts.[2] A fresh push for technological exchanges between the two states was also extended to include some sensitive military and defensive contracts, one of which involved the purchase of Israeli radars and rocket interceptors by South Korea.[3]

Overt deeper ties to Israel could indicate that the ROK was no longer worried about potential implications of such relationship on the Palestinian issue, which was once a major bugbear of South Korea's foreign policy toward the broader Middle East region. And unlike its East Asian neighbors, Japan and China, the ROK was not also obsessed with playing a mediating role in the complicated and knotty matter of the peace process involving

---

1 "S. Korea Pushes to Buy 10 Low-altitude Radars from Israel," *Yonhap New Agency*, April 9, 2014; "Israel's Innovations Have Korea, China Turning to Silicon Wadi," *Bloomberg*, July 9, 2014; "S. Korea, Israel Discuss Greater Cooperation," *Korea Herald*, December 23, 2014; and "Korea, Israel Teaming up on Drones," *Korea Joongang Daily*, June 21, 2016.
2 Ministry of Foreign Affairs (the Republic of Korea), *Diplomatic White Paper 2016*, pp. 206–207.
3 "South Korea Eyeing Israeli Rocket Interceptor - Manufacturer," *Reuters*, August 10, 2014; "S. Korea Sends Anti-piracy Troops to Gulf of Aden," *Yonhap News Agency*, February 9, 2015; and "South Korea Eager to Expand Ties with Israel," *Arutz Sheva*, March 10, 2015

the Palestinians and Israelis.[1] South Korea's real position with regard to the issue was already crystal clear to many, and its participation in any mediating efforts here and there could hardly help either party. Nor it did really stay the ROK's hands from forging diplomatic as well economic connections to Lebanon and especially Jordan.[2] The kingdom of Jordan has actually been on fairly good terms with South Korea, receiving a considerable amount of grants and loans from the East Asian country. Moreover, some Korean companies such as Hyundai have managed to capture a significant share of Jordan's markets in different areas.[3]

Compared to other states in the Levant region, nevertheless, Syria remained, as usual, the riddle of South Korean foreign policy. Only a handful of countries currently do not have any formal diplomatic relationship with the ROK, and one of them is Syria, which has always refused inflexibly to set up political ties with South Korea. Successive Korean governments before Park tried to enter the Arab country at least economically; a relentless policy which led to the creation of a business center by KOTRA in Syria in November 2009. The opening of the center, which was celebrated with a relatively great fanfare by some government officials and business leaders from both countries, buoyed up many in the ROK, who pinned their hopes on economic and technological means as a powerful instrument to eventually forge close normal political and commercial connections to Damascus.[4] But Syria was soon plunged into an internecine and protracted civil war that dashed hopes of a quick and quid pro

---

1 "Park Briefs Top Officials on Outcome of Middle East Trip," *Korea Herald*, March 13, 2015.

2 "Korea, US in Dialogue over NK, Iran," *Korea Herald*, August 21, 2014; and "Jordan, S. Korea Set Stage for Further Cooperation," *Jordan Times*, December 17, 2015.

3 "Korean Firm Gets Approval from Jordan's Cabinet for Oil Development," *Yonhap News Agency*, March 8, 2013; "S. Korea Pledges 1.2 tln Won in Overseas Aid for 2015," *Yonhap New Agency*, May 5, 2014; and "Hyundai Motor Group Bets Big on Middle East," *Korea Herald*, April 22, 2015.

4 "S. Korea Seeks Ties with Syria," *Korea Times*, February 2, 2009; "Korea's First Business Center in Syria Opens," *ROK's Ministry of Culture, Sports and Tourism*, November 17, 2009; and "Syria Denies Visa to S. Korean Chemical Weapons Inspector," *KBS*, December 18, 2013.

quo deal on close political and economic interactions between South Korea and Syria.[1]

A vocally staunch support of the anti-Assad forces by the Korean government made things much worse so that Syria even denied a visa to a South Korean national who was member of an international team dispatched to inspect the Middle East country's chemical weapons. Given this history of suspicion and mistrust, it seems unlikely that an Assad-led political system would easily let in South Korean contractors, many of whom are already waiting in the wings to flock into the war-torn country for lucratively massive construction contracts in a post-conflict Syria.[2] This is one reason why the Korean government under Park gradually yet quietly reconsidered its policy toward the Syrian civil war especially when the prospects for a swift removal of Assad from power, by either domestic forces or outside powers, dwindled year after another. Instead, the ROK shifted its attention to the rising ghost of the Islamic State (IS or ISIL) which was now supposed to pose greater dangers to South Korea's vested interests.[3]

The alarm bells were beginning to ring more loudly in Seoul when the IS included South Korea in the list of potential targets for its attacks worldwide.[4] Because of hosting US military bases, the ROK could actually encounter such a nightmarish scenario, a reality which soon forced the Park government to take some cautious measures against the threats posed by the IS.[5] Of course,

1 "S. Korea Pledges US $1 Million in Humanitarian Aid for Syrian Opposition," *Yonhap News Agency*, March 30, 2012; "S. Korea Hosts Meeting on Rebuilding Syria," *KBS*, December 12, 2013; and "Korea Accepts 200 Syrian Refugees," *Korea Times*, November 18, 2015.
2 "Korea Requests Further Participation in US$40 Billion UAE Infrastructure Projects" *Business Korea*, May 21, 2014; and "Overseas Construction Orders Won by S. Korean Builders Up 35 pct in 2014," *Yonhap News Agency*, June 2, 2014.
3 "East Asia Summit to Warn on IS Threat," *Bangkok Post*, November 10, 2014; "South Korea Fears Extremist Pull on Unhappy Youths," *Nikkei Asian Review*, February 5, 2015; and "More Koreans May Have Joined Islamic State," *Korea Times*, June 1, 2015.
4 "ISIS Reaches Korea," *Korea Joongang Daily*, January 21, 2015; "Korea's 135000 Muslims Fear Distrust after Paris Attacks," *Korea JoongAng Daily*, November 17, 2015; and "Islamic State Designates Korean Targets," *Korea Joongang Daily*, June 20, 2016.
5 "Seoul Voices Support for Obama's Plans to Strike Islamic State," *The Hankyoreh*, September 12, 2014; "ISIS Has Tanks and Missiles Made in

South Korea's main direction of foreign and security policy as a close ally of the United States could still bring grist to the mill of IS for such eventuality.[1] On top of that, many in South Korea worried that the US administration might again force South Korea to dispatch its military forces to the Middle East for an imminent ground operation under an American command to uproot the IS. Since the East Asian country was already paralyzed by a whole host of prickly problems at home and abroad, a new controversial adventure by its military forces in the topsy-turvy world of the Middle East region was the last thing the Park-led Korean government wished to deal with.[2]

North Africa: A changing politico-economic environment

South Korea has by and large been a newcomer to North Africa, and generally, to the African continent. Although the first Korean diplomats and political envoys to the Middle East had a chance to visit the region in the late 1950s, nonetheless, the ROK did not subsequently manage to build strong political and economic connections to North Africa.[3] As a matter of fact, South Korea's diplomatic ties to North Africa's most important country, Egypt, is a tale of roughly two decades old. But the ROK does not bear the whole responsibility alone. As former colonies with their own peculiar tormented history, North African countries, Egypt in particular, were not really interested in forging good relations with South Korea as a close ally of the United States.[4] They were instead in favor of close and multifaceted connections to the former Soviet Union and some other communist and socialist countries such as China and North Korea. That is

---

N. Korea," *Chosun Ilbo*, December 5, 2014; and "'Comfort Woman' Meets IS Sex Slave," *Korea Times*, May 29, 2017.

1 "Middle East's Misery and South Korea–Japan Peace," *Donga*, February 12, 2015.

2 "Editorial: Korea No Longer Safe," *Korea Herald*, November 19, 2015; and "IS Targets US Military in S. Korea and Citizens," *Korea Times*, June 19, 2016.

3 "How Deep Can South Korea–Africa Relations Go?" *Modern Diplomacy*, April 6, 2017.

4 "South Korea's Economic and Trade Offensive in North Africa," *North Africa Post*, March 1, 2013.

one reason why Pyongyang, rather than Seoul, could for decades enjoy close political and military interactions with Cairo.[1]

Political and ideological factors were, therefore, playing a part in putting a stop to the ROK's larger political and economic presence in North Africa, though South Korea could still capture a relatively good share of the Libyan construction market during its bubble days. Moreover, the Koreans, who were primarily interested in ready and safe opportunities in other parts of the Middle East, considered North Africa to be incognito to them and potentially hazardous. North Africa, and Africa in general, captured the attention of the ROK seriously only when previous lucrative opportunities in other exotic regions began to dwindle. From now on, South Korea's high agenda in the region incorporated various objectives, from extracting critical natural resources in Libya and snatching investment contracts in Tunisia to obtaining consumer markets in Egypt and exploring a potential free trade agreement with Morocco.[2] These critical priorities pushed the ROK government to beef up its politico-economic diplomacy, making North Africa into a new destination for occasional, and sometimes frequent, visits by successive South Koreans presidents, foreign ministers, and other top officials.

Park personally did not visit North Africa, but she met their leaders on the sidelines of the annual UN meetings in New York. She also once hosted the Egyptian president el-Sisi, who paid an official visit to the ROK in March 2016.[3] Among all North African countries, therefore, South Korea gave preference to Egypt because of its geographic location, demographic size, and cultural weight, hoping that the Arab country might provide better opportunities for the participation of Korean companies in its large scale economic and development projects.[4] Besides serving

---

1 "Korean People will Stand Firmly by the UAR, Syria and Other Arab Peoples," *Pyongyang Times*, June 8, 1967, p. 8.

2 "Egypt to 'Export' Stray Dogs to Korea: Report," *Korea Times*, December 13, 2016; and Daniel J. Schwekendiek, *South Korea: A Socioeconomic Overview from the Past to Present* (Abingdon and New York: Routledge, 2017), pp. 269–270.

3 "Egypt's Sisi Meets S. Korea Leader in Last Stop of Asian Tour," *Ahram Online*, March 3, 2016.

4 "Samsung, HAS to Invest $100m in Egypt: Ministry of Industry and Foreign Trade," *Daily News Egypt*, March 15, 2014; "Korea's Vice Defense Minister Leaves for Egypt," *Korea Herald*, March 27, 2017; and "S. Korea,

potentially as a convenient center to transfer Korean manufactured products to the neighboring countries, Egypt was also approached by the ROK for military deals and even cultural initiatives (e.g., the establishment of a culture center in Cairo in 2014 that was a first of its kind in the Middle East). The Park government aimed particularly to turn Egypt into one of South Korea's prospective customers for arms and military equipment such as K-9 howitzer through negotiating a defense deal with Cairo.[1]

What particularly stoked new economic expectations among Koreans about Egypt, and other countries in the region, was the so-called "Arab Spring," which had started in North Africa. It was a general belief among many observers and pundits that the political crisis had a lot to do with woeful economic conditions such as high unemployment rates in the region. They ineluctably came to the conclusion that the post-crisis political systems and national governments had little option but to do something serious with their economies through pork barrel spending on development programs and social welfare projects, implementation of which required active participation of many foreign companies such as those from the ROK. Putting strong faith in prophecies of this genre, a number of Korean companies started carving out their plans in the early months of the "Arab Spring."[2] Libya was a particularly alluring candidate for many Korean contractors who optimistically believed that the post-crisis Arab country would certainly provide another construction boom for the Koreans.

Succumbing to soothsayers and their sanguine views of new Libya, the Korean government soon emerged among the ardent proponents of anti-Gaddafi coalition.[3] Gaddafi had previously offered very generous contracts to the Koreans, but his demise

Egypt Ink Deal on Defense Cooperation," *Yonhap News Agency*, March 29, 2017.

1 "Korean Investment in Egypt Unswayed by Arab Spring," *Korea Times*, May 31, 2015; and "Egypt Interested in Buying K-9 Howitzer," *Korea Times*, July 26, 2017.

2 "South Korean Companies Shelve Libya Projects as Workers Flee Riots," *The Christian Science Monitor*, February 24, 2011; and "Korean Builders See Boon from Arab Spring," *Chosun Ilbo*, May 27, 2011.

3 "South Korea Gives for $1m to Libya Stabilization Projects," *Libya Herald*, November 24, 2016; and "S. Korea Extends Travel Ban on Iraq, Syria, Yemen, Libya, Somalia, Afghanistan," *Korea Times*, January 3, 2017.

was now on the wish list of almost every major Korean contractor.[1] Moreover, the ROK became one of the few countries in the world which kept its embassy running in Tripoli until its building fatally came under attacks in April 2015, forcing the Park government to temporarily transfer its diplomatic staff to the neighboring country, Tunisia.[2] South Koreans had, therefore, predicted a smooth and speedy process into an imminent economic boom fraught with bankable opportunities for their companies under a post-Gaddafi political establishment. But in sharp contrast to such heady optimism, Libya was driven into a bloody civil war with rival factions and forces from different parts of the country all engaging in turf battles to one day successfully and single-handedly take control of the entre territory and its plentiful resources.

Conclusion

The push for achieving a second boom was the main plank of South Korea's Middle East foreign policy under Park Geun-hye. This high objective certainly played a determining role in rekindling the ROK's politico-economic policies as well as cultural measures toward almost all Middle Eastern countries, but the recrudescence of a new boom in the region, as Koreans perceived it, was not eventually viable. There are by and large three reasons why another Mideast boom was hard to come by under current circumstances. First, oil prices on average remained low, putting a lot of budgetary pressures on all energy exporting countries in the region. Unlike in the first boom period, the Mideast countries had little appetite to allocate more funds for new development plans and welfare programs in the absence of satisfactory energy incomes, while some nations even had to shelve for now some of their ongoing projects because of financial uncertainty and budgetary constraints. Iran, as the biggest export market of South Korea in the Middle East, was undergoing additional dif-

1 "Libya to Grant 30-Day Tourist Visas to Koreans," *Korea Times*, October 31, 1986, p. 2.
2 "S. Korea's Embassy in Libya Attacked by Gunmen," *Korea Herald*, April 12, 2015; "Gunmen Attack South Korea Embassy in Tripoli, Two Local Employees Dead," *Reuters*, April 12, 2015; and "South Korea to Close Libya Mission," *China Daily*, April 16, 2015.

ficulties because a fair part of the Persian Gulf country's external revenues had been dammed up outside its sovereign borders due to sundry international sanctions.

Second, the Koreans themselves, both as professionals and laborers, contributed significantly to the materialization of the first boom. Korean companies were generally content with any small contract they could sign in the region, and many of them were prepared to work as subcontractors for more experienced and sophisticated corporations hailing from the West or Japan. Moreover, hundreds of thousands of Korean manual laborers in the Middle East were among the most hardworking and disciplined workers the region had ever encountered, and their strenuous life-styles and frugal saving habits back in those days had a lot of material benefits for their own country. But both groups have undergone tremendous transformation since then. Rich and resourceful Korean companies are now more risk-averse and finicky, giving their preferences and priorities to investments in highly rewarding and fail-safe environments. And while Korean laborers in the first boom were resolutely prepared to work some sixteen hours a day in the sweltering summers of Saudi Arabian deserts to advance the first boom dream, many of their children and grandchildren are no longer willing to spend even half of that time studying in air-conditioned spaces in Seoul or Busan.

Finally, Korean companies and businesses throughout the Middle East have run into a swarm of new international as well as local rivals that were largely non-existent over the course of the first boom. It is true that the Koreans could offer excellent financing packages and various types of advanced technology to their clients in the region, but other less well-known competitors have been striving to catch up by presenting more tempting deals and adequate qualifications. Many of these challenging contenders also adhere to some of the business traits and working ethics that once greatly contributed to the overall success of Korean companies in the Middle East. Additionally, an increasing number of local and regional players active in the critical political and economic affairs of the Middle East have undeniably become a powerful new force to reckon with. Be they more educated and sophisticated decision-makers or ambitious and experienced businessmen, the local and regional challengers have regarded themselves as more entitled to the windfalls of a potential second boom in the Middle East region.

CHAPTER 4. NORTH KOREA: SEEKING NORMALCY SINCE THE
DEMISE OF KIM IL-SUNG

The Democratic People's Republic of Korea (DPRK) is located quite far away from the Middle East as North Korea's remoteness from its nearest friendly partner in the region is a distance of more than 6,000 kilometers. Pyongyang and the political capital of any Middle Eastern country appear to be far more distant when the two sides have to deal with each other through the existing sea lines of communication. Moreover, the East Asian state and almost all countries in the Middle East share very little in common in terms of the pivotal political, economic, and cultural characteristics with which they are generally associated. Although North Korea and most of the Middle Eastern nations are situated in the larger Asian continent, politico-economic as well as socio-cultural differences between them are truly contrasting. On top that, the DPRK's relatively small geographic size and even a smaller economic weight would conventionally hamstring it from becoming a major player in the rather complex and topsy-turvy politics of the Middle East region.

In spite of the foregoing impediments, however, the DPRK's relationship with the Middle East has been widely publicized particularly during the past two decades. North Korea's somewhat friendly connections to and official interactions, often miscellaneously, with the region have been constrained only to a small number of countries over the course of several decades, but the nature and scope of such engagement has usually been reported in a way that makes its presence in the entire Middle East appear almost incessant and omnidirectional. Deep down, the North Korean–Middle Eastern relations have long been potentially susceptible to misperception, misinterpretation, misreport, overstatement, and exaggeration. This problem only aggravates when the academic community in the world tends to by and large shun away, for whatever reason, from conducting its own unprejudiced and inquisitive inquiry into the dynamics of the DPRK's relations with the Mideast countries, while a deluge of press coverage and media reports on the subject here and there often takes advantage of every chance to as usual fill the void.

In essence, North Korea's engagement in the Middle East is a narrative of some six-decade long developments. Neither the DPRK in East Asia nor its Middle East partners have remained standstill over this time span as each respective region has undergone significant changes and transformation. In particular, the leadership of the North Korean communist system is now in the hands of the third generation. No matter how stagnant and monolithic it may seem at first sight, each generation has certainly experienced its share of commitments, attachments, and adjustments.[1] It is then plausible to argue that every generational change of leadership in Pyongyang would have certainly had some repercussions on the East Asian country's approach toward its Middle Eastern partners, even if some of those implications were perceived to be a kind of policy response by North Korea to the developments initially taken place in a Mideast country. This chapter attempts, therefore, to probe the twists and turns in the DPRK's interactions with the Middle East since the death of Kim Il-sung, beginning with an analytical appraisal of some priorities and preferences dear to each leadership generation in North Korea, and how they could potentially influence

---

1 Bruce W. Bennett, *Preparing for the Possibility of a North Korean Collapse* (Santa Monica, CA, and Washington, D.C.: Rand, 2013); and John Sweeney, *North Korea Undercover: Inside the World's Most Secret State* (New York: Pegasus Books, 2015).

Pyongyang's overall orientation toward its different partners in the region.

Adapting to change: From idealism to pragmatism

As the architect and symbol of the North Korean political establishment, Kim Il-sung certainly played an indispensable role in carving out major initial foreign policies of his communist country toward different parts of the world, including the Middle East. Under his indisputable and domineering leadership, the DPRK commenced its official and unofficial contacts with the Middle East at a critical time when the Cold War calculations of diplomacy and realpolitik greatly influenced the mindset and actions of policymakers in both regions. Ideational attributes and ideological affinities were, therefore, very decisive factors in the nature and scope of North Korean presence in the Middle East. That is a main reason why the communist Asian state managed to set up friendly diplomatic relationship only with a few number of socialist and left-wing leaning countries throughout the Middle East. Of course, Pyongyang was still willing to engage some other countries in the region on pure economic terms, but such policy inclination had little chance to trump the ideology element.[1]

After all, the personal characteristics of Kim Il-sung as well as the national economic system which he supervised had significantly contributed to that eventuality. Kim Il-sung was a man of conviction, and there was a long narrative for his legitimacy claim and ideological streak, dating back to the years he was steadfastly leading the guerrilla fights to liberate his fatherland from the Japanese colonizers.[2] Middle East countries, especially North Korean close partners in the region, had thereby very little doubt about Kim Il-sung's ideological beliefs and political rhetoric which by and large had the ultimate say in Pyongyang's approach toward the outside world. With regard to economics, the DPRK was not really in a desperate position during the initial decades of Pyongyang's interactions with the Middle East

---

1 "Korean Trade Del. Back from Arab Nations," *Pyongyang Times*, February 24, 1966, p. 1.
2 Paul French, *North Korea: The Paranoid Peninsula – A Modern History* (London and New York: Zed Books, 2005), p. 9.

when even South Korea lagged behind its communist rival in the north almost by every economic yardstick. Whether it was for the self-reliance and autarky policy of *Juche* or some other justifications, the relatively positive economic conditions at home made it possible for the North Korean leadership under Kim Il-sung not to fundamentally forsake its ideological attributes and political orientation in favor of potentially lucrative trading and commercial interests in the Middle East.

Unlike Kim Il-sung, his son and successor Kim Jong-il was not fortunate with regard to those two important factors. He was devoid of any personal charisma, while his ideological principles and genuine political commitments could hardly impress North Korea's staunch allies in the communist world let alone its partners in the Middle East. In spite of his formal communist attire and gestures, Kim Jong-il was never heard to utter any Mideast-related statement worthy of attention that would give them confidence as to his rather peculiar ideational proclivities and ideological allegiance. Economically, Kim Jong-il was far more exposed to perils simply because North Korea under his leadership continuously experienced hardship and wretched conditions.[1] Coupled with natural disasters like droughts or extreme floods, the economic circumstances of average North Korean citizens aggravated as various types of assistance and grants supplied through some of the former communist allies of Pyongyang dwindled to a trickle by the time Kim Jong-il consolidated his power base within the political establishment of the DPRK.

Kim Jong-il was, moreover, preoccupied heavily with the domestic affairs of North Korea epitomized by his *Songun* (military-first) politics. He was susceptible to imminent domestic plots and betrayal from the very first day he took on the top leadership in Pyongyang, compelling him to perpetually keep a beady eye on every move of his subordinates across the political spectrum, so that he could not pay close attention to what was really going on in every nook and cranny of the world as his father had

---

1 Michael Breen, *Kim Jong-il: North Korea's Dear Leader* (Hoboken, NJ: John Wiley, 2004), p. 174.

used to do.[1] Unlike his father, who visited the Middle East and held summit meetings with his counterparts from the region, Kim Jong-il was too busy domestically to either make an official trip to a Mideast country or to host the leader of an important partner from the Middle East, even supposing that he personally had a zealous interest to do so.[2] Additionally, during the period when Kim Jong-il was ruling the roost in Pyongyang, the Middle East in general and some North Korean partners in the region in particular, underwent significant developments which required the officials and policymakers in Pyongyang to take into account the new circumstances in order to vouchsafe their pivotal interests there.

Under a much younger and inexperienced Kim Jong-un, who unexpectedly and prematurely replaced his father in late December 2011, the DPRK had to further tap into practical, rather than ideational, foreign policies and strategies so that Pyongyang could benefit better from connections to the old as well as the newly-made partners throughout the Middle East. Kim Jong-un's own personal beliefs in carrying out some necessary domestic economic reforms to boost the living standards of North Korean citizens upped the ante for the diplomatic corps of the DPRK to engage the Middle East in more practical terms.[3] A combination of internal and external parameters, therefore, worked to gradually dilute the ideological facets of North Korean overall approach toward the region, no matter if the DPRK still attached to some of its well-known official rhetoric when

---

1 Steven Denney, Christopher Green and Adam Cathcart, "Kim Jong-un and the Practice of Songun Politics," in Adam Cathcart, Robert Winstanley-Chesters, and Christopher K. Green, eds., *Change and Continuity in North Korean Politics* (Abingdon and New York: Routledge, 2017), pp. 53–64; and Richard Worth, *Kim Jong Il* (New York: Chelsea House, 2008), pp. 69–70.

2 "Korean People will Stand Firmly by the UAR, Syria and Other Arab Peoples," *Pyongyang Times*, June 8, 1967, p. 8; and "His Excellency Nureddin al-Atassi Pays State Visit to the DPRK," *Pyongyang Times*, October 6, 1969, p. 1.

3 Paul French, *Our Supreme Leader: The Making of Kim Jong-un* (London: Zed Books, 2016); and Adam Cathcart, "Kim Jong-Un Syndrome: North Korean Commemorative Culture and the Succession Process," in Adam Cathcart, Robert Winstanley-Chesters, and Christopher K. Green, eds., *Change and Continuity in North Korean Politics* (Abingdon and New York: Routledge, 2017), pp. 6–22.

dealing with a Mideast-related issue here or there.[1] But what is then the scope and size of transformation in North Korea's foreign policy toward the Middle East, and how did Pyongyang eventually come up with some new measures to implement its rekindled approach in different parts of the region?

Iran: The triangulation comes full circle

When the DPRK approached Iran for the first time in the second half of the 1960s and precisely after April 1967 when the ROK opened its embassy in Tehran, the communist East Asian country was bearing all the hallmarks of a revisionist revolutionary state. It was also a time when North Korea needed to appear nice to its Middle Eastern counterpart, while there happened to be little at stake, if any, for a relatively pragmatist and conservative Iran to rush into forging friendly diplomatic ties with Pyongyang then. Later, when the Islamic Republic moved hurriedly into the communist state's open arms despite its "neither the East, nor the West" rhetoric at home, the Iranian officials conveniently eclipsed their North Korean counterparts in terms of ideological credentials and ideational attributes.[2] In recent years, however, things have pretty much reversed course; Pyongyang seems to be once again in great need of courting Tehran partly because of a slew of regional and international constraints put on the communist state, while Iran is confidently and assertively coming out of the cold with little, if any, passion for keeping close connections to countries such as North Korea.[3] There has been, therefore, three distinctive periods in the North Korean–Iranian relationship with relatively similar ups and downs in the dynamics of their bilateral interactions over the past several decades.

---

1 Patrick McEachern, *Inside the Red Box: North Korea's Post-totalitarian Politics* (New York: Columbia University Press, 2010), p. 248.
2 "Davat koreye shomali az Iran baray moghableh ba America" [North Korea Invites Iran to Confront America], *Aftab Yazd*, October 17, 2017, p. 15.
3 Tim Beal, *North Korea: The Struggle against American Power* (London: Pluto Press, 2005); and Andrew S. Natsios, *The Great North Korean Famine: Famine, Politics, and Foreign Policy* (Washington, D.C.: United States Institute of Peace, 2001), p. 125.

Both North Korea and Iran looked the other way where it came to the ideational and ideological affinities with which each country was affiliated during the first period of their relations that lasted roughly half a decade under the monarchical dynasty of Pahlavi.[1] The DPRK generally did not criticize the main approach and direction of the Iranian foreign policy and its international alliance politics, preferring to instead highlight certain positive domestic developments taking place in the economic and social realms then.[2] The Iranian government also seemed to be in fine fettle as long as the ideological rhetoric of the communist state was to eventually materialize the long dream of Korean unification. Materially, the DPRK was buying energy resources from Tehran, while Iran was willing to engage in low-profile commercial activities with Pyongyang by importing some of its minerals.[3] By and large, the depth and pace of their relations were lackadaisical, and that is why Iran had to handle the country's connections to the DPRK through its Beijing embassy even when North Korea had already set up a fully-functioning embassy to manage its diplomatic and commercial activities in Tehran.

In the second period, North Korea becomes all of a sudden a cynosure of attention as the Islamic Republic neglects its fervent ideological orientation by making overtures to the communist leaders of the DPRK chiefly for arms deals.[4] The outbreak of the Iran–Iraq War and inaccessibility to the well-stocked markets of military equipment had left the Iranian officials with little option but to approach a number of card-carrying communist states such as North Korea and China in order to replenish their

---

1 Shirzad Azad, "Iran and the Two Koreas: A Peculiar Pattern of Foreign Policy," *The Journal of East Asian Affairs*, Vol. 26, No. 2 (Fall/Winter 2012), pp. 163–192.
2 David Alton and Rob Chidley, *Building Bridges: Is There Hope for North Korea?* (Oxford: Lion Hudson, 2013), p. 199; and Daniel Tudor and James Pearson, *North Korea Confidential: Private Markets, Fashion Trends, Prison Camps, Dissenters and Defectors* (North Clarendon, VT: Tuttle Publishing, 2015), pp. 129–144.
3 Charles K. Armstrong, *Tyranny of the Weak: North Korea and the World, 1950–1992* (Ithaca and London: Cornell University Press, 2013), p. 179.
4 For a brief and incisive sketch about some ideological commonalities and discrepancies between the Islamic and communist creeds, see: Bernard Lewis, "Communism and Islam," *International Affairs*, Vol. 30, No. 1 (1954), pp. 1–12.

swiftly draining reserves of weapons and munitions.[1] The DPRK even served as a conduit for the Chinese to ship their military equipment to Iran in the early years of the bloody war, though the arms which Pyongyang itself was selling to Tehran then were not all made by the communist Koreans themselves. After all, the arms deals were really lucrative enough for the Koreans, encouraging the communist officials of Pyongyang to double down their rhetoric on the non-religious ideational commonalities which they shared with their counterparts from the Islamic Republic.[2]

The end of the Iran–Iraq War in 1988, however, did not terminate the wartime cooperation between the two countries on conventional weapons. As Iran embarked on its unconventional defense systems after the conclusion of the military conflict with Iraq, North Korea could still maintain its cherished status among the Iranian officials intact by sharing with Tehran its technological know-how in the fields of missile and, probably, nuclear programs.[3] That is why the second period of bilateral interactions between Iran and North Korea was going to last for at least some three decades, making a number of major stakeholders around the world very queasy about the scope and extent of the two-way connections involving the Iranians and North Koreans. In spite of all speculations and guessing reports about the North Korean–Iranian collaborations throughout those years, nonetheless, the nature of their joint activities was symbiotic since the two parties could mutually benefit from sharing technical know-how or from bartering one service for a required commodity.[4] Of course, the official data about the true nature and volume of their interactions remained largely opaque as usual,

---

1 William R. Polk, *Understanding Iran: Everything You Need to Know, from Persia to the Islamic Republic, from Cyrus to Ahmadinejad* (New York: Palgrave Macmillan, 2009), pp. 190–191.

2 James Jay Carafano, "Implications of Iran Negotiations for North Korea," *The Journal of East Asian Affairs*, Vol. 29, No. 2 (Fall/Winter 2015), pp. 1–19.

3 "Iran Bought 18 North Korean Missiles," *Taipei Times*, December 17, 2005; "The Endless Iranian Nuclear Crisis," *Project Syndicate*, June 27, 2007; and "Exclusive: North Korea 'Secretly Helped by Iran to Gain Nuclear Weapons'," *The Telegraph*, September 9, 2017.

4 Bill Gertz, *The Failure Factory: How Unelected Bureaucrats, Liberal Democrats, and Big Government Republicans are Undermining America's Security and Leading US to War* (New York: Crown Forum, 2008), pp. 34–36.

leaving a number of other stakeholders and interested observers with little option but to make assumptions and, sometimes, wild conjecture.[1]

In the third period, which started about half a decade ago, the DPRK and Iran have engaged each other under rather different circumstances. The communist state of East Asia has encountered mounting international pressures, tightening regional isolation, and increasing domestic problems, forcing its top elites and policymakers to approach their foreign friends in the Middle East such as Iran on more practical terms.[2] They have even proposed new areas of pure economic cooperation, ranging from energy and fishery, in order to partially make up for their dire shortcomings at home.[3] On the other hand, the Iranian officials have been somehow coy to give any prominence to their relationship with the DPRK, choosing to often host their visiting communist counterparts behind the scene away from any sensational media attention and eye-popping news reports.[4] Few, if any, prominent politicians from Iran have been willing to plan for an official visit to the DPRK in recent years in spite of their occasional statements about the rationale and value of preserving good ties with North Korea.[5] If things moved in such direction, Pyongyang would risk becoming more of a liability for Tehran in the foreseeable future unless the two parties found new grounds for close collaboration beyond the realms of muni-

---

1 Bruce Bechtol, Jr., *The Last Days of Kim Jong-il: The North Korean Threat in a Changing Era* (Washington, D.C.: Potomac Books, 2013), p. 30.

2 "Kim Yong Nam Receives Credentials from Iranian Ambassador," *Korean Central News Agency (KCNA)*, February 2, 2017.

3 "The Iran Deal's North Korean Shadow," *Project Syndicate*, July 30, 2015; "Merkel Suggests Iran-style Nuclear Talks to End North Korea Crisis," *Reuters*, September 10, 2017; and Alison Behnke, *Kim Jong Il's North Korea* (Minneapolis, MN: Twenty-First Century Books, 2008), p. 91.

4 "Zarif dar goftegoo ba Newsweek: Komakhay koreye shomali dar jang tahmili ra faramoosh nakardehim" [Zarif in Talk with Newsweek: We Haven't Forgot North Korean Helps during the Imposed War], *Tabnak*, October 7, 2017; and "Sokhangooy vezarat kharejeh: Hamkari Iran va koreye shomali edameh peida mikonad" [Foreign Ministry Spokesman: Iran-North Korea Cooperation Continues], *Aftab Yazd*, October 19, 2017, p. 1.

5 Shirzad Azad, "Principlism Engages Pragmatism: Iran's Relations with East Asia under Ahmadinejad," *Asian Politics & Policy*, Vol 7, No. 4 (October 2015), pp. 555-573.

tions and missiles in which the Iranians are increasingly becoming assertive and self-reliant.[1]

The Gulf Cooperation Council: An incessant quest for economic gains

The political establishment of North Korea has over time transformed to resemble the dynastic systems which rule the member countries of the Gulf Cooperation Council (GCC). In addition to their perpetually monopoly of power and wealth, the hereditary rulers of both the DPRK and GCC states have almost always usurped the supreme authority in the land by riding roughshod over their entire subjects. Besides such political commonality, moreover, North Korea shares with the GCC states some other things in common, particularly where geography and history are concerned. Like most of the GCC countries, the political regime of the DPRK rules over a relatively small piece of territory despite its inflated and constant claims of legitimacy over the entire Korean Peninsula since the late 1940s. In terms of historical parallel, foreign powers have played an indispensable role in carving out the contemporary identities of North Korea and the sheikhdoms of the GCC, inflicting upon them a taxing obsession to perpetually worry about potentially insidious interferences of regional and international players in their internal and external affairs.[2]

It is probably no coincidence, therefore, why the DPRK strived unrelentingly from the 1960s onward to approach those Arab sheikhdoms some of which were to soon emerge as a sovereign states and later form the GCC bloc together. In spite of the fact that the two parties held diametrically opposed views in terms of international alliance systems, North Korea tried to forge at least some sort of economic connections to those Arab

---

1 "Doostani az jens Seoul ya Pyongyang" [Seoul or Pyongyang-Esque Friends], *Jahan Sanat*, August 27, 2017, p. 1. However, there have been some important changes in Tehran's behavior toward Pyongyang since the time the Trump administration withdrew unilaterally from the landmark JCPOA and imposed subsequently several rounds of crippling sanctions on the Persian Gulf country.

2 Charles Jr. Wolf and Norman D. Levin, *Modernizing the North Korean System: Objectives, Method, and Application* (Santa Monica, CA: Rand, 2008), pp. 7–9.

entities lying in the southern part of the Persian Gulf region.[1] The communist state of North Korea managed to thereby get a lot of economic benefits from those Arab sheikhdoms, especially Kuwait and Saudi Araba, from the 1960s through 1980s during which there was actually no official diplomatic relationship between them.[2] One effective strategy of the DPRK was to refrain from any sharp criticism directed at those Arab kingdoms' foreign policies and international alliance orientation, focusing instead on some other innocuous and harmless areas such as cultural matters while reporting about or addressing its counterparts in the region.[3]

The end of the Cold War, nevertheless, forced the DPRK to rekindle its long quest for establishing official diplomatic ties with the GCC states. Pyongyang had lost a significant number of its allies and close partners in the erstwhile communist bloc, while the flow of various types of economic and non-economic assistances supplied to North Korea by those states gradually decreased to zero so that even Russia and China were now demanding full and ready payment for their energy exports to Pyongyang.[4] The North Korean perseverance paid off over time as the communist country could set up by 2007 some sort of formal diplomatic relations with all GCC states except Saudi Arabia. The DPRK, moreover, managed to establish its only GCC embassy in Kuwait, using the diplomatic mission to handle the relationship with its Arab counterparts throughout the GCC bloc. The al-Sabah ruling family of Kuwait also let generously the DPRK's only airline, Air Koryo, to establish a direct flight between Pyongyang and Kuwaiti City, facilitating travels particularly for many North Korean laborers working in various GCC countries.[5]

---

1 "Korean Trade Del. Back from Arab Nations," *Pyongyang Times*, February 24, 1966, p. 1.

2 Nihon Boeki Shinkokai, *China Newsletter*, Volumes 49–65 (Tokyo: Nihon Boeki Shinkokai, 1984), p. 20.

3 "Congratulations to Kuwaiti People on their National Holiday," *Pyongyang Times*, February 26, 1977, p. 4.

4 Nicholas Eberstadt, *The North Korea Economy: Between Crisis and Catastrophe* (New Brunswick, NJ: Transaction Publishers, 2009), 115–116.

5 "A Look at the Kuwaiti–North Korean Relationship," *LobeLog*, February 9, 2017; and "Why the North Korea Crisis Has Serious

As a matter of fact, the situation of North Korean workers has by and large become the most controversial aspect of the DPRK's connections to the GCC countries in recent years. There has been a flurry of press and media reports about their grueling conditions and exploitation by local employers as well as by their North Korean brokers. There is no official statistics about the exact number of North Korean laborers in the region, but it is widely speculated that some ten thousands of them are working across the GCC, particularly in Kuwait, Qatar, and the United Arab Emirates (UAE).[1] Many of North Korean workers are basically hired for construction projects some of which contracted by South Korean companies. It is estimated that currently some 60,000 North Korean laborers are working in 20 countries of which Russia and China host 50,000 of those workers alone.[2] The history of Korean workers in the Middle East is not really new, harkening back to the mid-1970s onward when the first oil shock and the ensuing construction bonanza brought a swarm of Korean contractors and laborers to the region. As South Koreans gradually became financially rich and less willing to engage in manual and demanding works in the Middle East, their North Korean brethren could swiftly replace them if different political and diplomatic circumstances made it possible for them to do so.

Meanwhile, North Korean workers became a soft target of political tensions and regional rivalries involving a number of stakeholders here and there. The Trump administration in the United States pressured Kuwait to impose against North Korea certain diplomatic and economic punishments, which the al-Sabah rulers complied, largely pretentiously and temporarily, justifying their measures based on what the UN resolutions dictated because of the DPRK's missile tests.[3] The Japanese

Implications for the Middle East," *The National*, August 13, 2017.
1 "Thousands of North Korean Laborers in US-allied Gulf Nations," *Associated Press*, July 28, 2017.
2 "How North Korea Takes a Cut from Its Workers Abroad," *The Washington Post*, November 1, 2017.
3 "Kuwait Says North Korean Workers Welcome Then Refutes Itself," *Bloomberg*, August 11, 2017; "Four Countries Expel North Korean Diplomats," *Korea Joongang Daily*, September 19, 2017; and "Trump Administration Presses Kuwait on Qatar, North Korean Workers," *Los Angeles Times*, September 19, 2017.

government also dispatched its foreign minister, Taro Kono, to those GCC states which host a bigger number of North Korean workers in order to seek their cooperation with regard to the implementation of the sanctions levied against Pyongyang.[1] The Japanese were insisting that remittances of workers would supply grist to the mills of North Korea's missile and nuclear programs, endangering the security of their country.[2] Within the GCC bloc, moreover, the UAE accused the Qataris for abusing the North Korean laborers, while Qatar used its Doha-based influential *Al Jazeera* broadcaster to disclose a secret shipment of arms equipment which the rulers of Abu Dhabi had apparently purchased from Pyongyang for their military adventure in the ongoing Yemeni civil war.[3]

Iraq: The troublesome axis turns into a tacit nexus

The communist regime of the DPRK could set up diplomatic relationship with the socialist Ba'ath Party of Iraq in July 1968, though there happened to be some sort of informal political and economic connections during the run-up to the commencement of official relations between Pyongyang and Baghdad.[4] The two countries subsequently engaged in amicable interactions with each other until the outbreak of the Iran–Iraq War in 1980 when the Iraqi government of Saddam Hussein suddenly severed all ties with North Korea, accusing Pyongyang of not honoring its politico-diplomatic commitments to Baghdad by sneakily as-

---

1 "Kono Applauds Kuwait for Halting Visas to North Koreans," *The Asahi Shimbun*, September 11, 2017; and "Japan Seeks Arab League's Cooperation against North Korea," *Nikkei Asian Review*, September 12, 2017.

2 "Foreign Minister to Visit Mideast to Drum Up Pressure on N. Korea," *Kyodo News Agency*, September 8, 2017; and "Japan Urges Mideast to Stop Accepting North Korea Migrant Workers in Bid to Squeeze Funds to Pyongyang," *The Japan Times*, September 12, 2017.

3 "UAE Bought Weapons from North Korea for War in Yemen," *Middle East Monitor*, July 20, 2017; "The Strange Role North Korea Is Playing in the Gulf Crisis," *The Washington Post*, July 26, 2017; and "Gulf Rivals Accuse Each Other of N. Korean Ties," *The Straits Times*, July 28, 2017.

4 "Joint Announcement on Visit of Government Economic Delegation of Republic of Iraq to DPRK Issued," *Pyongyang Times*, November 6, 1971, p. 6; and "Korean Party and Gov't Del. Visit Iraq and Syria," *Pyongyang Times*, August 5, 1978, p. 2.

sisting Tehran.[1] The communist Koreans actually did not give a hoot about the allegation or the ruptured relationship with Iraq simply because the stakes from the newly-warmed up ties with Iran were so high that only the part of military deals between Tehran and Pyongyang was enough to be dubbed "a heaven-sent fortune" for the DPRK. But the wrath of the Ba'ath Party was so powerful and long-lasting that North Korea could not find any enthusiasm and verve to approach Baghdad for rekindling bilateral ties until the downfall of Saddam in 2003.

Despite a lack of any meaningful connections between the DPRK and Ba'ath Party, however, the US president, George W. Bush, singled out, quite out of the blue, North Korea and Iraq along with Iran in his notorious "axis of evil" address delivered in January 2002. The seriousness of Americans to topple the Ba'ath Party from power in Iraq particularly frightened the North Korean political establishment.[2] There were even some media reports that North Korea had offered, somewhat astonishingly, political asylum to Saddam and his family through a Hong Kong-based go-between with close connections to Pyongyang.[3] The DPRK had apparently thought of accommodating the Iraqi leader in a cloistered mountain in order to fend off an imminent military adventure of the Bush administration in the Middle East which could potentially spread out to include North Korea in Northeast Asia.[4] In another staggering news story, moreover, it was reported that the Saddam regime had dubiously transferred to the DPRK some $10 million for a North Korean missile technology just prior to the onset of the US-led military conflict against Baghdad in March 2003, but the Ba'ath Party of Iraq was never given a chance to receive the sensitive Korean equipment.[5]

1 "Iraq Breaks Diplomatic Ties with N. Korea, Syria, Libya," *Reuters*, October 11, 1980.

2 William Blum, *Rogue State: A Guide to the World's Only Superpower*, third edition (London: Zed Books, 2006), p. 22.

3 "Stanley Ho Claims North Korea Offered Dictator Asylum," *South China Morning Post*, March 2, 2003.

4 "Three Strange Links between Macau, North Korea: From Saddam Hussein to Customs Chief's Death," *South China Morning Post*, May 7, 2017.

5 "Iraq Paid N. Korea to Deliver Missiles," *The Washington Times*, October 4, 2003.

As far as purported international political ideology and orientation were concerned, nonetheless, there was relatively little ground for a hiatus of diplomatic interactions between North Korea and Iraq for decades. That is a reason why the DPRK kickstarted its diplomatic quest to forge official ties with Baghdad once the dust of the Iraq War and the following insurgency settled in most part of the Middle Eastern country. The new political regime that acceded to power in Iraq after the overthrow of Saddam and his Ba'ath Party was not disinterested at all in extending hands of friendship to North Korea; a mutual desire and understanding which culminated in restoring official diplomatic relationship between Pyongyang and Baghdad in September 2008. In such eventuality, however, the intermediary role of Iran needs not to be overlooked because Tehran was already enjoying from favorable and friendly connections to both Pyongyang and Baghdad. And this is exactly another "marvel" of the Iraq War which brought about a new nexus of mutual understanding and good relationship between all three countries, while there used to be bad blood between North Korea and Iraq as well as between Iraq and Iran prior to the collapse of Saddam and his Ba'ath Party in Baghdad.[1]

Turkey: Mending fences with the brethren's brothers

The contemporary history of Turkey's relationship with the Koreans on both sides of the 38th parallel is somewhat complicated, fuzzy, and significant. It all goes back to the internecine conflict of the Korean War during which Turkey emerged as an important participant in support of the Republic of Korea (ROK). Among major countries which entered the war in favor of the ROK, Turkey suffered one of the highest percentages of losses as some three thousands of its military forces were either killed or maimed over the course of the three-year war. Turkey's war casualties actually exceeded those from Australia, Canada, and France all of which got involved in the conflict backing South Korea. Moreover, Turkey was the only country that joined the Korean War from the greater Middle East region. Within

---

1 Hal Brands, *From Berlin to Baghdad: America's Search for Purpose in the Post-Cold War World* (Lexington, KY: University Press of Kentucky, 2008), p. 304.

the larger Turkish society, however, the move was very controversial from the beginning because a majority of the citizenry
had no inkling about the urgency and necessity behind their
country's participation in a major military confrontation taking
place on faraway territories.

Meanwhile, Turkey's gambit in the Korean War paid off as
the country was soon rewarded generously by its inclusion in
a number of US-backed critical clubs and communities such as
the North Atlantic Treaty Organization (NATO). The war adventure also cemented Turkey's close relations with South Korea until the present day, giving Ankara a special place in Seoul's
overall foreign policy approach to a wider Middle East region.
That is no coincidence why in the late 1950s and early 1960s
Turkey practically became a toehold of sorts through which
the ROK could approach many other Mideast countries for the
establishment of diplomatic relationship.[1] Moreover, many top
officials from South Korea and Turkey are used since then to often call each "brothers," though such genteelism has some other
deeper historical as well as cultural roots and goes far beyond
the narratives of the Korean War.[2] Non-governmental connections, and especially academic and tourism sections, between
the two countries have also been equally affected by such an
ostensibly demonstration of camaraderie and *esprit de corps* at
higher political levels.[3]

It was, therefore, a concoction of the foregoing factors which
nipped in the bud any possibility of diplomatic relationship between the DPRK and Turkey until the beginning of the 21st century. Pyongyang and Ankara eventually normalized their official
ties in January 2001 through signing a Memorandum of Understanding (MOU) in Beijing. In particular, Turkey justified its
action by highlighting the importance of formal relations with
North Korea for the peace and stability of the Korean Peninsula
as well as the Middle East region. Still, the political capital of

---

1 ROK's Ministry of Foreign Affairs, *Wegyo Munseo* [Diplomatic
Archives] (Seoul: Ministry of Foreign Affairs, 1996).
2 "Turkey — Brother Nation of Korea," *Korea Times*, November 15, 2015;
and "Turkey and South Korea: Blood Brothers for 60 Years," *Anadolu
Agency*, November 18, 2015.
3 "Turkey, South Korea Celebrate 60 Years of Exemplary Diplomatic
Relations," *Daily Sabah*, March 8, 2017.

neither country was prepared to host a dazzling diplomatic mission of the other party as the Turkish embassy in Seoul was dubiously assigned the task of handling North Korean affairs, while the DPRK's Sofia-based embassy was accredited to the Middle East nation. On top of that, the two countries have been rather cautious and heedful in their official bilateral interactions with each other since then, though Turkey has not been shy to boast about its occasional humanitarian assistance to North Korea.

The Levant: From military involvement to cautious observation

North Korea's engagement in the Levant region (consisting of Syria, Lebanon, Jordan, and Israel) has uninterruptedly lasted for more than half a century. Syria has been the closest and most loyal partner for the DPRK in the region through all the ups and downs. In the beginning, Syria's struggle for the Arab Cause (the Palestinian issue) and North Korea's zealous campaign in favor of the Korean Cause (the unification of the peninsula) cemented significantly a bilateral relationship which was to survive until the present day. The ideological as well as political foundations of Pyongyang–Damascus were initially so strong that the DPRK was prepared to even partially assist Syria militarily during its violent conflict with Israel over the Palestinian issue, though a number of other Arab states, Egypt in particular, were involved in the bloody battle as well. In addition to their friendly diplomatic and political relationship, the two countries soon managed to broaden their close cooperation into a number of other areas, ranging from arms to agriculture.[1]

Because of its precious regional circumstances and constrained international access to arms markets, the socialist regime of Syria was especially in need of developing better military connections to the communist regime of the DPRK. Such critical collaboration in conventional armaments between the two countries were later extended to include some unconventional arms such as missile, chemical, and probably even nuclear technologies. But the Syrians were a relatively cash-strapped nation

---

1 Stephan Haggard and Marcus Noland, *Famine in North Korea: Markets, Aid, and Reform* (New York: Columbia University Press, 2007), p. 32.

and did not possess much material and financial resources to make their North Korean partners happy in long haul particularly when Pyongyang badly needed some economic incentives to keep in motion its devoted all-out ties with Damascus.[1] This was especially the case when Syria was plunged into an internecine civil war over the past several years during which the DPRK adapted a cautious approach by refraining to assist the al-Assad regime through active and direct military means, though Pyongyang was never afraid of throwing its full diplomatic and political support behind Damascus.[2]

North Korea's relationship with the Palestinians has generally followed a similar trajectory. In the heyday of their companionship and comradeship, the DPRK was willing to dispatch its military forces to fight the Israelis in favor of the Palestinians. North Korea, moreover, developed good connections to the Palestinian Liberation Organization (PLO), training its forces to wage a successful guerrilla warfare against the Jewish state. But as the Palestinians themselves and a number of Arab states engaged in peace process negotiations with Israel, the DPRK lost its motivation to campaign for the displaced and hopeless Arabs. Pyongyang still had many reasons to swiftly recognize the newly-proclaimed state of Palestine, but its lackadaisical approach to the Palestinian political authorities stemmed partially from working closely with the Hezbollah of Lebanon.[3] Iran was again an important factor behind such interactions because a great deal of the training and equipment which the Hezbollah could receive from the Koreans had to be bankrolled by Tehran.

In comparison, North Korea has long been steadfast in its own standoffish attitudes toward Israel. The DPRK was hardly shy to approach either Lebanon or Jordan to establish bilateral diplomatic relations, but Pyongyang never wished to set up such connections to the Jewish state. Of course, the East Asian coun-

---

1 David Albright, *Peddling Peril: How the Secret Nuclear Trade Arms America's Enemies* (New York: Free Press, 2010), p. 4.

2 "N. Korea Boasts Friendship with Syria amid Global Fury over Chemical Weapon Attack," *Korea Times*, April 7, 2017; and "Being Neighbors with North Korea in the Middle East," *Anadolu Agency*, September 12, 2017.

3 Bruce E. Bechtol, *Red Rogue: The Persistent Challenge of North Korea* (Washington, D.C.: Potomac Books, 2007), pp. 46–47.

try's close ties to a number of relatively like-minded partners throughout the Middle East greatly contributed to its antipathy, and initial belligerence, toward Israel.[1] And in spite of its larger politico-ideological orientation to designate the Jewish state as an "imperialist satellite" installed by the West in the region, Pyongyang had still another justification to keep Israel at arm's length one decade after another. Like many of their brethren in the southern part of the Korean Peninsula, the communist Koreans in the North have long considered the Jews as a culprit behind the partition of their territories in the 1940s and the ensuing miseries for millions of people on both sides of the Demilitarized Zone (DMZ).[2]

For its part, Israel has left no stone untouched in taking advantage of North Korea's connections to the Levant in particular, and the Middle East in general. In addition to perpetually putting in the crosshairs every single aspect of Pyongyang's interactions with the region, the Israelis have often overplayed the North Korean factor in the international relations of the Middle East in order to give more credence to their own perpetual claims of susceptibility and vulnerability.[3] By nominally seizing the moral high ground, the Jewish state has even sometimes found the matter a timely excuse to divert regional and international attention from the implications of its measures taken against Syria, the Palestinians, and the Hezbollah.[4] Moreover, Israel has not been shy to exploit the DPRK–Middle East relationship in order to curry favor with other stakeholders in the West as well as in the East.[5] Such behaviors and tactics have on occasion led

---

1 "Israel 'Occupying Curse on Middle East', Says North Korea," *The New Arab*, April 30, 2017.

2 Ronald Meinardus, "Anti-Americanism in Korea and Germany: Comparative Perspectives," in David I. Steinberg, ed., *Korean Attitudes toward the United States: Changing Dynamics* (Armonk, NY: M.E. Sharpe, 2005), pp. 80–89, "Why Is South Korea So Anti-Semitic?" *The Diplomat*, May 15, 2014; and "Pro-North Korean Website in Los Angeles Promotes anti-Semitism," *Jewish Journal*, July 12, 2017.

3 "Iran–North Korea Nuclear Collaboration Is Israel's Worst Nightmare, Says Expert," *Jewish Journal*, November 7, 2017.

4 Adrian Buzo, *The Guerilla Dynasty: Politics and Leadership in North Korea* (London and New York: I.B. Tauris Publishers, 1999), p. 196.

5 "The Korean Peninsula is not the Middle East," *People's Daily*, April 28, 2017.

to the provocations which other more nonpartisan and disinterested Israelis have deemed "irresponsible" and "dangerous."[1]

North Africa: Hitting a brick wall

The history of the DPRK's official interactions with North Africa is somehow older than its relationship with the rest of the Middle East. The North Korean policy toward the region was initially part of its broader approach toward the African continent. Pyongyang could receive significant solidarity and moral support from African nations particularly at a period when the Korean Cause had the enthusiastic endorsement and strong backing of many countries throughout the continent. The communist East Asian country was also able to make up for their empathy and cooperation partially through offering aids and development assistances especially in those years when the North Korean economy was experiencing its halcyon times.[2] Still, the DPRK had many good reasons to over time forge closer ties with North Africa than the rest of the continent. And despite the fact that Algeria became the first country from North Africa to recognize the DPRK, nonetheless, Egypt and Libya turned out to be closer partners with which North Korea developed stronger ties for several decades to come.[3]

North Korea and Egypt set up their official diplomatic relations in 1963; more than three decades before Cairo officially recognized South Korea in 1995. A close affinity between the two countries, however, began to germinate almost from the time Nasserism stormed into power in Cairo from 1952 onward. The DPRK particularly made history when it strongly supported Egypt over the Suez Crisis of 1956, and contributed to the Arab country a small amount of financial assistance which was symbolically very significant. In 1967, Pyongyang once again threw its full diplomatic support behind Cairo during the Six-

---

1 "N. Korea Threatens Israel after Liberman Calls Kim a Madman," *The Times of Israel*, April 29, 2017.
2 Robert Daniel Wallace, *North Korea and the Science of Provocation: Fifty Years of Conflict-Making* (Jefferson, NC: McFarland & Company, 2016), p. 202; and "Why the North Korean Economy is Growing," *The Economist*, June 27, 2017.
3 Bechtol, *Red Rogue*, p. 16.

Day War with Israel.[1] When the Yom Kippur War broke out in October 1973, the communist regime of the DPRK upped the ante by sending its pilots to the conflict in favor of Egypt and its Arab allies. Such impressive and glaring background was thereby very conducive to further boost the North Korean–Egyptian relations under the presidency of Hosni Mubarak who ruled the Arab nation for some three decades (1981–2011). As a sign of mutual understanding and symbiotic relationship between the two countries, Mubarak visited North Korea four times from 1983 to 1990 alone.[2]

True that Egypt became a major customer of North Korea's military equipment and missile technology under Mubarak, however, the two parties managed over years to develop their relations into a number of other rewarding economic and commercial activities. As a case in point, an Egyptian telecommunications company named Orascom assisted North Korea to create its own cellphone network of Koryolink in 2008 only a few years before Mubarak was toppled from power. Under his main successor, General el-Sisi, Egypt has come under mounting pressures, especially by Washington, to at least rein in its arms deals with Pyongyang. By resorting to arm-twisting tactics such as withholding military or other types of aids to Egypt, the United States under the Trump administration has revved up its retaliatory measures to curtail Pyongyang's financial gains from its beneficial connections to Cairo. When push came to shove, nevertheless, the el-Sisi government announced that the Arab country was willing to suspend its military interactions with North Korea. But the capture of the Cairo-bound freighter, *Jie Shun*, as the "largest seizure of ammunition in the history of sanctions against the DPRK" had already made it clear that Egypt was not really going to forgo permanently its long-established connections to Pyongyang simply because of some temporary diplomatic pressures exercised by Washington or Seoul.[3]

---

1 "The Egypt–North Korea Connection," *The Diplomat*, August 28, 2017.
2 Yonhap News Agency, *North Korea Handbook* (Armonk, NY: M.E. Sharpe, 2003), p. 979.
3 "Facing US Pressure, Egypt Cuts Military Ties to North Korea, Report Says," *The Boston Globe*, September 12, 2017; "Yonhap Report: Egypt Cuts Military Ties with North Korea," *The Asahi Shimbun*, September 13, 2017; and "A North Korean Ship Was Seized Off Egypt with a Huge Cache of

With regard to Libya, the DPRK's relations with the North African country is by and large constrained to the reign of its former strongman, Colonel Muammar Gaddafi. Under his leadership in Libya the two parties developed close relationship from the early 1970s onward. Such camaraderie and affinity between the two countries personified by signing a defense treaty in 1982, making Libya the only country in the world besides the Soviet Union and the Communist China which entered into such critically sensitive partnership with the DPRK. In fact, the clout of the communist country in Libya was so domineering that South Korea failed for many years to come into terms with the Gaddafi regime over setting up official diplomatic ties between the two countries, though Seoul still managed to dispatch a number of its major contractors to implement some construction projects for Tripoli. As a corollary to such friendly attachment, the relatively cash-awash regime of Gaddafi became a big buyer of the DPRK's exports of conventional military munitions as well as missiles to the wider Middle East region.[1]

North Korea's good fortunes in Libya, however, came to an end abruptly in 2003 when the Gaddafi regime entered into a precarious agreement with the West to terminate permanently its dogged and hell-for-leather pursuit of nuclear weapons and advanced missile technologies. Consequently, Libya had to soon axe its military deals with the DPRK and even dismantle those SCUD C missiles which Tripoli had already purchased from Pyongyang at a whopping cost.[2] Of course, such unfavorable developments did not pull the plug on the North Korean–Libyan bilateral connections in some other areas; such eventuality was not to occur even when the more than four-decade long regime of the castrated colonel collapsed like a bolt from the blue in 2011. After all, a pertinent perk was that the communist regime of the DPRK emerged as one of the first countries in the world to swiftly take a leaf out of Gaddafi's blue book by steadfastly clinging to its own constant quest for nuclear and missile tech-

---

Weapons Destined for a Surprising Buyer," *The Washington Post*, October 1, 2017.
1 Bechtol, *Red Rogue*, p. 97.
2 Charles L. Pritchard, *Failed Diplomacy: The Tragic Story of How North Korea Got the Bomb* (Washington, D.C.: Brookings Institution Press, 2007), p. 135.

nologies regardless of a recent US policy to force Pyongyang into a Libya-esque submission.[1]

Conclusion

The international system has undergone tremendous developments since the time the DPRK first approached its agreeing partners in the Middle East. North Korea made overtures about either setting up or improving diplomatic relationship with Middle East countries in the heydays of the Cold War, and a great deal of Pyongyang's long-lasting connections to the region were initiated during that critical period. The communist regime of the DPRK was certainly a valuable asset for its Cold War patrons so that the Chinese, and even the Soviet Russians, were for a while at the whim of Pyongyang to ship furtively their arms to Tehran. But there has been much water under the bridge since then partly because once the bipolar world was eventually consigned to history and a new system of, quote-unquote, 'multipolarity' was in gestation to eventually replace it, almost all great powers had already carved out their own unique approaches and links to a wider Middle East region. Under such new circumstances in the international system, therefore, North Korea had to reevaluate gradually certain politico-ideological elements of its Middle East policy in order to vouchsafe its interests in the region in long haul.

While the structure of world politics was in the throes of seismic changes, moreover, Middle East countries were subjected to transformation. A number of them went through a regime change, and some other countries readjusted their broader foreign policies and strategies to deal with what new pressing circumstances at home and abroad dictated them to do so. North Korea was to be ineluctably affected by such developments. In the early decades of the DPRK's interactions with the region, for instance, Middle East nations had little, if any, significant vested interests in East Asia, but a new 'looking-East' orientation has for some time become a buzzword of influential foreign policy and economic circles in many Mideast countries. To make itself

---

1 "North Korea Cites Muammar Gaddafi's 'Destruction' in Nuclear Test Defence," *The Telegraph*, January 9, 2016.

to these pivotal policy changes, therefore, North Korea needed to extend its critical connections to the Middle East into new areas other than bargains over conventional and unconventional arms which had now become, by and large, about pleasing dollars than political doctrines.

Finally, transition in the top political leadership of the DPRK had its own ramifications for the East Asian country's broader agendas toward the Middle East. Under the first generation, North Korea's motions and gestures to its counterparts in the Middle East were quite sincere, and summit meetings and personal contacts between the heads of states or governments were at all-time high. A bulk of the bilateral interactions among the two parties concentrated on high politics. Such attitudes and trends shifted steadily when the second and especially third generations of political leadership took the helm in Pyongyang. Coupled with other external and internal parameters, the weltanschauung and personal preferences of the second and third generations were certain to influence how the DPRK previously conducted its Middle East affairs. As a corollary, North Korea's overall approach toward the Middle East has generally become more mature and multifaceted, though Pyongyang has done little to chip away at the suspicion of other stakeholders about the nature and scope of its somewhat anomalous connections to the region.

Chapter 5. Unknown And Undetected: Taiwan's Resilient And Viable Approach

The Republic of China (ROC) or the island of Taiwan, for-merly known as Formosa, is a relatively small country with a demographic size of roughly 23.5 million people. It is duly rec-ognized as a functioning sovereign state only by a group of tiny countries, most of which are located in the Pacific and Carib-bean islands. Although Taiwan used to be officially a normal, close partner of many countries in different parts of the world including the Middle East, back a couple of decades ago, a pa-riah status thrust forcefully upon it in the international system since the 1970s has tremendously increased its involuntary isola-tion and contraction. As a corollary to that, the ROC is not really well-known to most of the world population, and their major developments — and even their location — are by and large ig-nored by influential international media and press.[1] Moreover, Taiwanese manufactured goods and services have often been susceptible to such eventuality even when their abundant quan-tity and sterling quality could comfortably stay on par with their better recognized rivals from the East or the West.

When it comes to the Middle East, Taiwan is particularly burdened. In spite of the fact that the ROC once enjoyed offi-

---

1 Christopher M. Dent, *The Foreign Economic Policies of Singapore, South Korea and Taiwan* (Cheltenham, UK: Edward Elgar, 2002).

cial and cordial diplomatic relationship with a number of major Middle Eastern countries, today not a single country in the region holds formal political connections to Taipei. Of course, Taiwan is relatively far away from the region geographically as the distance between the ROC and the nearest political capital of a major Mideast country is more than 4,000 miles (6,437 km), and the sea route is even longer. But the issue is not distance or even size alone, since there are many other small Eastern and Western countries which are significantly farther away than the ROC and yet they seem to be popular and present in the region.[1] Taiwan is off the radar screens in any important international news coverage throughout the Middle East, its history and present identity are hardly ever taught at schools, and most Mideast citizens have essentially no idea what the ROC ultimately stands for.

No matter how unfamiliar and strange Taiwan might seem, however, it has had an enduring presence in the region over the past several decades. And regardless of all ups and downs, its interactions with the region have actually been multidirectional, straddling political, economic, technological, cultural, and even military spheres. How then did Taiwan manage for so long to cope with its own subterranean existence in the topsy-turvy world of the Middle East and engage the region in all those areas? What underpinned the foundation of Taiwanese policies toward the Middle East, and what was at stake that forced Taipei to strive to achieve its objectives in the region? Is it plausible to credit and discredit Taiwan alone for all of its triumphs and troubles in the Middle East? What is the role of other stakeholders? This chapter seeks to answer such compelling questions by surveying the nature and scope of the ROC's multifarious interactions with the Middle East over the course of more than six decades.

---

1 Ian Taylor, "Taiwan's Foreign Policy and Africa: The Limitations of Dollar Diplomacy," *Journal of Contemporary China*, Vol. 11, No. 30 (2002), pp. 125–140.

Precarious Security: From the Taiwan Straits to the Hormuz Straits

From the time the nationalist forces of General Chiang Kai-shek and their civilian supporters retreated to the island of Taiwan in 1949, the survival and safety of the Taiwanese formed the cornerstone of the ROC's policies at home and abroad. At least for some four decades, Taipei adhered to its rigid "one-China policy," claiming that it was the legitimate representative of all the Chinese territories and had the authority to wield power over all Chinese people including those living in mainland China. Even when Taiwan was shaken to the core on October 25, 1971, by a U.N. vote to expel it from the international body in favor of communist China, the ROC still resolutely claimed its legitimacy over China, before the small island country eventually adapted a more flexible politico-diplomatic position on this matter around 1988.[1] Throughout those chaotic and dangerous decades when Taipei had to fight for that noble cause politically and occasionally militarily, however, the East Asian state had to work on a parallel to turn its sovereign constituency into a role model economically, technologically, and socio-culturally.[2]

The ultimate goal was to achieve rapid economic development and turn the ROC into a productive powerhouse in Northeast Asia. Such a key objective also became a linchpin of the Taiwanese grand strategy, linking economic progress and technological advancement to its status on the world stage. If the country faced any significant deficit in political and diplomatic terms, therefore, economic achievements and technological betterment at home were thought to effectively make up for some other limitations and shortcomings the Taiwanese citizens had to bear with.[3] The island country had carved out

---

1 The move was interpreted by many in the West as a betrayal of Taiwan and selling out the island in favor of potentially huge promising opportunities to be tapped in the Communist China. For more details, for instance, see: Jeffrey A. Engel, ed., *The China Diary of George H.W. Bush: The Making of a Global President* (Princeton, NJ: Princeton University Press, 2008), pp. 144, 295.
2 Joel Atkinson, "China–Taiwan Diplomatic Competition and the Pacific Islands," *The Pacific Review*, Vol. 23, No. 4 (2010), pp. 407–427.
3 Murray A. Rubinstein, "The Evolution of Taiwan's Economic Miracle 1945–2000: Personal Accounts and Political Narratives," in Douglas

its essential economic policies and the pertinent strategies at a critical time when the rival Maoist China had badly busied itself with ideological preoccupations.[1] As a corollary to that, the ROC's economy found its momentum to move through the gears in the 1960s, providing a propitious ground for the Taiwanese lightning-quick transformation in economic, technical, social, and cultural realms unprecedented in the entire history of the Chinese people.

Meanwhile, the ROC's ambitious economic and technological goals only upped the ante as the island country was already experiencing a dicey situation with regard to its basic prerequisites to survive in long haul. Located geographically at a relatively hostile environment, Taiwan was not really endowed with either sufficient natural resources at home or easy access to those crucially-needed materials in its immediate neighborhood. Of course, the ROC was long at the whim of the United States for much of its military and defense requirements, but what the ambitious agenda of economic development ultimately entailed was a horse of a different color. Taipei's military reliance on Washington was a bilateral matter which could be sorted out partly because the Americans had themselves put the defense of the critical island country at the heart of their strategic policies in the region.[2] In comparison, the onerous agenda of industrialization and economic development was by any measure a greater task, the implementation of which required the ROC to do its own heavy lifting.

To successfully carry out its economic development projects, the ROC needed to connect to as many friendly regions and nations as possible no matter how arduous, and sometimes frustrating, the undertaking was going to be. Even when its erstwhile allies and close partners had to switch their allegiance one

---

B. Fuller and Murray A. Rubinstein, eds., *Technology Transfer between the US, China and Taiwan: Moving Knowledge* (Abingdon and New York: Routledge, 2013), pp. 25–46.

1 Earl C. Ravenal, "Approaching China, Defending Taiwan," *Foreign Affairs*, Vol. 50, No. 1 (1971), pp. 44–58.

2 Victor Marchetti and John D. Marks, *The CIA and the Cult of Intelligence* (New York: Knopf, 1974); and Dennis Van Vranken Hickey, *Foreign Policy Making in Taiwan: From Principle to Pragmatism* (Abingdon and New York: Routledge, 2007), p. 6.

by one from Taipei to Beijing, Taiwan still had little option but to work discretely in order to secure its rapidly expanding interests.[1] Exporting of manufactured goods was just as daunting a task as bringing in goods that the ROC needed, as the island nation's maritime borders were difficult to secure. Taiwan obviously had fewer problems dealing with its Japanese or American counterparts for a whole host of imported or exported goods, but interactions with some other regions could entail many complications.[2] And among those other essential regions in the world, the Middle East was particularly vital to the ROC's grueling patterns of industrialization and economic development.

Although the Middle East could certainly be a lucrative market for Taiwanese manufactured goods, it was the ROC's desperate dependence on imported energy resources that determined the region's value to Taipei. The more Taiwan grew economically, the more dependent it became on Mideast oil, making energy security a critically important concern. On top of that, the Middle East was far away and its topsy-turvy affairs could only exacerbate the situation, forcing the government in Taipei to keep a lookout with regard to securing its energy requirements. Coupled with its own national anomalies, such anxiety and obsession formed a delicate security nexus which stretched from the Straits of Taiwan to the Straits of Hormuz.[3] In order to cope with its urgent security concerns in the Middle East, therefore, the ROC needed to as much as possible forge close connections to the region, straddling all political, economic, technological, cultural, and even military realms.[4]

---

1 J. Bruce Jacobs, "One China, Diplomatic Isolation and a Separate Taiwan," in Edward Friedman, ed., China's Rise, Taiwan's Dilemma's and International Peace (Abingdon and New York: Routledge, 2006), pp. 85–109.

2 Deon Geldenhuys, Isolated States: A Comparative Analysis (New York: The Press Syndicate of the University of Cambridge, 1990), p. 418.

3 "US Lauds Taiwan for Limiting Iran Ties," Taipei Times, December 6, 2012, p. 3.

4 "The Imports and Exports of the ROC in the Middle East," Sino-Arabian Association Bulletin (Taipei), No. 66 (1986), p. 34.

Political Links: From Full Normalization to Subterranean Attachment

The ROC's political experiences in the Middle East preceded the takeover of the mainland by the Maoist Chinese and the ensuing withdrawal of Chiang Kai-shek's loyal forces to Taiwan. As a case in point, Chiang had personally visited Egypt in November 1943 to attend the Cairo Conference which led to the signing of the Cairo Declaration he then dubbed "the greatest triumph in the history of China's foreign affairs."[1] After their retreat to the island of Taiwan in 1949, practical experiences and lessons gleaned previously in the Middle East helped the Chiang-led Chinese nationalists to swiftly develop relatively close and friendly ties with many countries in the region. Moreover, their knowledge and record in the region gave the Taiwanese a head start in Middle Eastern affairs as compared to some of their East Asian rivals who possessed little, if any, first-hand experiences in the region. For instance, when the Republic of Korea's (ROK) first good-will mission was travelling to a number of Middle East countries in 1957, the Taiwanese diplomatic envoys in the region turned out to became instant gurus for their visiting Korean partners, educating them about some basic yet critical practical information about the Middle Eastern politico-economic and cultural issues.[2]

Many Mideast countries were equally cognizant of Taiwan's attention to the region, and they were thereby receptive to its politico-diplomatic gestures. This was particularly the case among those major Middle Eastern countries that had allied themselves with the US-led camp *vis-à-vis* the communist bloc. Iran before 1971 and Saudi Arabia before 1991 were particularly prominent examples. Under the Pahlavi dynasty, Iran actually developed a very close and cordial relationship with Taiwan which lasted for more than two decades before Iran switched its diplomatic allegiance to Maoist China.[3] When the Iranian mon-

---

1 Jay Taylor, *The Generalissimo: Chiang Kai-shek and the Struggle for Modern China* (Cambridge, MA: Harvard University Press, 2000), p. 256.
2 Shirzad Azad, *Koreans in the Persian Gulf: Policies and International Relations* (Abingdon and New York: Routledge, 2015).
3 James A. Bill, *The Eagle and the Lion: The Tragedy of American–Iranian Relations* (New Haven and London: Yale University Press, 1988), p. 155.

---

arch paid an official visit to Taiwan in June 1958, as the first ever visit to the island country by a non-Asian leader, the Shah of Iran received a hero's welcome through the streets of Taipei. In May 1971, moreover, the Saudi leader, King Faisal, was another top Mideast official who paid a high profile visit to Taiwan. Given the fact that Taiwan was simultaneously undergoing significant developments internationally, the visit by the Saudi leader then conveyed critical political messages.[1]

More importantly, Saudi Arabia refused to swiftly ditch Taiwan for immediate political and economic advantages offered by the communist Chinese. While many countries throughout the Middle East region, like other parts of the world, gradually normalized their bilateral relationship with Beijing at the cost of Taipei from 1971 onward,[2] Saudi Arabia did not succumb to such prevailing trend in spite of all signs which indicated that the ROC had little chance, if any at all, to get back its erstwhile international status.[3] Interestingly, after Oman and Libya normalized their diplomatic relationship with Beijing in 1978, Saudi Arabia became the only Arab country that still insisted on maintaining its full diplomatic ties with Taiwan for more than a decade to come. Because of such anomaly, therefore, the ongoing political connections to Riyadh practically became the most important pattern of Taipei's international relations until the early 1990s when Saudi Arabia backed down by establishing diplomatic relations with Beijing.[4]

From 1991 onward, economic and cultural representatives and offices became very instrumental in the ROC's both official and informal interactions with many Middle Eastern countries, including Saudi Arabia. Not only Taiwan turned some of its previous embassies and consulates in the region into economic and cultural bureaus, a number of Mideast countries also either used

---

1 "Taiwan Could Provide a Powerful Example for US–GCC Relations," *The National*, May 13, 2015.
2 "Taiwan, Israel, Western Sahara not Invited to AACC," *The Jakarta Post*, April 20, 2015; "Burkina Faso Severs Ties," *Taipei Times*, May 25, 2018, p. 1; and "Editorial: Diplomatic Policy Needs Explaining," *Taipei Times*, May 25, 2018, p. 8.
3 "The Saudi Connection," *Far Eastern Economic Review*, July 9, 1982, pp. 28–29.
4 "Saudi Arabia–Taiwan Relationship Built on Common Values," *The China Post*, September 22, 2011.

the same tactic or simply set up from the scratch such offices in Taipei. Even Iran offered at some point to establish its own commercial representative office in Taipei, though the idea was turned down by the Taiwanese foreign ministry because of some political pressures wielded by other stakeholders. These critical economic and cultural representatives, no matter how small-scale in size or subterranean in nature, could function like an embassy, providing opportunities for both Taiwanese low-profile officials and their Middle Eastern counterparts to exchange views and finalize deals without enraging any important political official in Beijing.

In particular, the forgoing approach turned out to be an important element in Taiwan's critical yet behind-the-scenes connections to Israel over many decades. Almost until the early 1990s, the Arab–Israeli conflict was a hot-button issue in the international relations of the Middle East–East Asia.[1] Even some major US allies such as Japan and South Korea were walking on eggshells while dealing with their Arab counterparts in the region. Compared to their Japanese and Korean allies, the Taiwanese were obviously more vulnerable with regard to the simmering Arab–Israeli disputation. Such vexing situation thereby compelled Taipei to behave more cautious than Tokyo and Seoul in the Middle East so that the island state's growing vital interests in the region, the crude oil supply in particular, was not going to be threatened or held back by the Arab–Israeli issue. By keeping its tactful ties to Tel Aviv on the hush-hush, the Taiwanese orientation proved eventually to be way more successful than what many observers and pundits expected as Taipei's subterranean yet sensitive areas of cooperation with and connections to the Jewish state were hardly effected by its real position toward the contentious Arab–Israeli matter in the Middle East.[2]

There were, nevertheless, other metrics by which to evaluate Taiwan's perpetual attention to politics and generally all po-

---

1 "Israel Would Object to Closer Taiwan–Iran Ties," *The China Post*, July 26, 2010.
2 Jonathan Goldstein, *Jewish Identities in East and Southeast Asia: Singapore, Manila, Taipei, Harbin, Shanghai, Rangoon, and Surabaya* (Berlin and Boston: De Gruyter Oldenbourg, 2015), pp. 82, 100.

litical occurrences in the Middle East.[1] Considering themselves a victim of international power politics, many in Taiwan used to often draw their own lessons by sizing up crucial developments in a region which has long been regarded as an incestuous hothouse of realpolitik involving external stakeholders. The region was astonishingly never short of providing an example in any political or non-political issue germane to the situation of the ROC.[2] The Taiwanese could sometimes compare their own country to an isolated and sanctioned Iran which had unfairly come under tremendous international pressures and mistreatments for close to four decades.[3] In other occasions, small Middle Eastern states like a besieged Qatar or independence-seeking aspirants like the Kurds in the region could conjure up promptly melancholic memories of hardships and dashed dreams the people in Taiwan had gone through for several decades.[4]

The Prime Target: Economic Interests

Taiwan's growing commercial connections to the Middle East was first and foremost a natural ramification of its breakneck economic developments at home. What later became known as the "Taiwan Miracle" (*Táiwān Qíjì*) in the 1970s and 1980s had its pivotal roots in the high-speed growth and industrialization programs of the late-1950s which helped the ROC to emerge as one of the "four Asian Tigers" and a model of modernization and development in a broader context.[5] Although all such critical economic and social developments played an indispensable role in cultivating business and profit-oriented activities

1 Surprisingly, the ROC even captured the attention of the Islamic State in the mid-2010s, when the extremist religious group in the Middle East gave a demonstration of the Taiwanese flag fleetingly. "Taiwan Attends Anti-Islamic State Coalition Meeting in Brussels," *Focus Taiwan*, December 4, 2014; "Defense Ministry Aware of ISIS Video Showing Taiwan's Flag," *Focus Taiwan*, November 24, 2015; and "Taiwan Gets Unwanted Recognition from IS," *BBC News*, November 26, 2015.
2 "Taiwan's Trade Delegation Meets with Saudi Businessmen," *Arab News*, October 19, 2011.
3 "Editorial: The Cost of Independence," *Taipei Times*, October 5, 2017, p. 8.
4 "Qataris' Strategy a Blueprint for Taiwan," *Taipei Times*, November 8, 2017, p. 8.
5 John F. Copper, *Taiwan: Nation-State or Province?*, third edition (Boulder, Colorado: Westview Press, 1999), p. 169.

between Taiwan and its partners in the Middle East, nonetheless, the island country's delicate political situation ineluctably rendered its domineering impacts as well. Since the ROC was cognizant of its growing political isolation particularly from the early 1970s onward, fostering better commercial interactions with some highly-political regions like the Middle East could partially make up for the island state's deteriorating politico-diplomatic hiccups here and there. Moreover, an increasing level of economic relationship with the Mideast countries could better assure Taiwan's rising stakes in the wake of its dwindling political connections to the region.[1]

Over decades, therefore, the importation of fossil fuels, crude oil in particular, became consequently a major characteristic of the ROC's expanding trade and commercial interactions with the Middle East. In fact, when Taiwan's state-owned oil company, the Chinese Petroleum Corporation (CPC), began importing crude oil directly from Saudi Arabia in June 1973, it sowed the seeds of a new trend in the Taiwanese–Middle Eastern relations that has never stopped until the present day. Various powerful political developments such as the oil shocks and the ensuing anxieties over the energy security forced Taiwan to diversify its sources of crude oil supplies, but Taipei almost always relied on the region for a bulk of its required energy demands.[2] By and large, some one-third of the ROC's oil needs had to be constantly supplied by the "swing producer," Saudi Arabia, though Taiwan had skillfully developed significant energy deals with a number of other countries in the region, including Iran which at once was providing some four percent of the ROC's crude oil imports.[3]

In addition to the policy of diversification in the main purveyors of its oil supplies, Taiwan also needed to bring variety to the

---

1 "The Recent Situation of the Oil Export of the Middle East States to Taiwan," *Sino–Arabian Association Bulletin* (Taipei), No. 21 (1979), p. 4.
2 International Business Publications USA, *Taiwan: National Security and Defense Law Handbook*, fourth edition (Washington, D.C.: International Business Publications USA, 2008), p. 15.
3 "Taiwan Cuts 2011 Iran crude Imports by Nearly Half," *Reuters*, February 20, 2012; "Taiwan Exempted from US Sanctions on Iran Oil," *Taiwan Today*, June 13, 2012; and "Taiwan Keen to Boost Oil Imports from Iran by 27%," *Tehran Times*, April 9, 2016.

very energy basket the East Asian country continuously strived to satisfy.[1] A pertinent strategy was, therefore, to look after new sources of clean energy so that the ROC could simultaneously meet its energy requirements and anti-pollution pledges. Indonesia for some times became a major provider of Taiwan's importation of liquefied natural gas (LNG), but the developing country of Southeast Asia itself soon joined many other energy consumers in the world, forcing Taipei to once again tap into the preternatural reserves of the Middle East for its increasingly growing LNG demands.[2] The Persian Gulf country of Qatar was obviously the main choice in the region which could comfortably take the place of Indonesia in filling up sufficient number of LNG cargoes bound for Taiwan. The United Arab Emirates (UAE) and Oman were other Middle Eastern countries which later emerged as the secondary sources of the LNG imported into the ROC.[3]

Energy imports certainly formed the backbone of Taiwan's trade ties with the Middle East, but Taipei's relationship with the region was never a one-way business. Long-term trade data and statistics show that the ROC could engage in bilateral commercial interactions with almost all countries and political entities throughout the Middle East region, including the Palestinians as well as Syria and Yemen both of which are currently in the throes of civil wars.[4] Interestingly, some Taiwanese products experienced their heydays in Iran when the Persian Gulf country came under sever international sanctions and financial restrictions which provided a fertile ground for off the books economy and sub-rosa trade.[5] Various types of Taiwanese goods were

---

1 "Saudi Arabia Threatens to Stop Oil Exports to Taiwan," *Khaleej Times*, May 12, 2008; "Taiwan Halts Iran Imports," *Oil & Gas News* (Manama), June 18, 2012; and "Troubled Taiwan Shipping Line Cuts Iran Service," *Financial Tribune*, April 23, 2017.

2 Taiwan Bureau of Energy, *Energy Statistics Handbook 2010* (Taipei: Taiwan Bureau of Energy, Ministry of Economic Affairs, 2010).

3. "Saudi-Qatar's True Battleground Is Asia," *Bloomberg*, June 6, 2017.

4 "Saudi Arabia Invites Taiwan to Help Develop Economic City," *The China Post*, March 2, 2008.

5 "Taiwan Tries to Cut Iranian Oil Imports at Behest of the US," *Taipei Times*, February 9, 2012, p. 1; "Taiwan Welcomes Implementation of Iran Nuclear Deal," *Focus Taiwan*, June 10, 2014; and "Interview with Brian Hook: We Call Iran Regime What It Is – A 'Kleptocracy'," *Al Arabiya*, January 12, 2019.

thereby smuggled into the bustling bazaar of Iran through the neighboring territories such as Turkey and especially the entrepôt Dubai.[1] This was a major reason behind an upswing in the ROC's exports to the UAE, though the tiny Arab country had equally become a rendezvous for many other Eastern and Western products which were waiting in their wings to be smuggled into Iran through both formal and informal channels.[2]

In spite of their relative technological sophistication and price advantages, the Taiwanese brands did not capture a proportionate share of the markets in the region as compared to their rivals from other East Asian countries such as Japan, the ROK, and later mainland China. Taiwan had been burdened with major political impediments and legal obstacles, and that is why the ROC's diplomats and official envoys could not freely engage in marketing and promotional activities for Taiwanese companies and businesses in the region, while their East Asian counterparts hardly missed any propitious opportunity to facilitate the ground for further infiltration of their own nation's brands into this or other Middle Eastern country. Of course, the ROC's major companies and private businesses were not entirely blameless in this matter either. Due to their risk-averse proclivities and cultural preferences, most of them were in favor of pouring their hard capital into safe and up-and-coming places like the mainland China as a zeitgeist of international investors and entrepreneurs.[3]

Battling the Bottleneck: Technology Transfer

Although some Middle Eastern countries are now putting a heavy emphasis on the matter of technological transfer while engaging in substantial business deals with their Western and Eastern partners, however, the history of this trend goes back at least to the 1970s when a sudden hike in petroleum prices in the

1 "Taiwan Foreign Ministry Denies Rejecting Iran Trade Office Request," *The China Post*, May 26, 2010; "Taipei does not Oppose Business with Iran: MOFA," *Taipei Times*, August 1, 2010, p. 3; and "Taiwan's Overtures toward Turkey," *Cihan News Agency*, May 31, 2014.
2 "Taiwanese Shipping Line Berths at Iran's Shahid Rajaee Port as Sanctions Eased," *Trend News Agency*, July 22, 2014.
3 Graham Field, *Economic Growth and Political Change in Asia* (New York: St. Martin's Press, 1995), p. 40.

wake of the first and second oil shocks generated huge revenues for all oil exporters in the region. Buoyed up by wads of ready cash, the oil-rich countries of the region thereby embarked upon massive infrastructure projects, turning the Middle East all of a sudden into one of the most promising places in the world for construction works, engineering goods, and technological services.[1] Contractors and engineers from the West and the East all were dragged into the region to get their fragrant share of the Mideast's blossoming boom which in some parts of the region like Saudi Arabia was to last until the mid-1980s. In return for the financial rewards secured through a successful implementation of the signed contracts, foreign companies and entrepreneurs were logically expected to bring in their own expertise and technical know-how.[2]

As compared to some of their East Asian counterparts, the Koreans in particular, the Taiwanese were not seen to be actively involved in the region during the first Mideast boom. Moreover, some Taiwanese had gone to the region then in order to collaborate with the Japanese or Western companies as subcontractors and labor force, though the number of the Taiwanese who had hired themselves out as manual laborers in the Middle East were not that significant at all (interestingly, Taiwan itself later became a destination for some of the workforce of the Southeast Asian countries who had been taken to the Middle East during the first oil boom of the 1970s and 1980s). Still, those companies from the ROC which carried out projects independently in the Middle East during those boom years were largely constrained to Saudi Arabia where a more favorable political environment could help them to win some large and lucrative deals. As a case in point, a Taiwanese heavy construction corporation, Ret-Ser Engineering Agency (RSEA), managed to sign a number of profitable Saudi projects valued around $1.3 billion over a decade starting in 1973. The Taiwanese company managed to carry out projects for the Saudis, ranging from highway to housing and from swage system to industrial park. The Jubail Fertilizer was

1 John Bunton, "Western Contractors Face New Challenges," *Middle East Economic Digest (MEED)*, April 1979, pp. 3–5.
2 James Buchan, "The Meaning of Competition," *Saudi Business*, February 1, 1980, pp. 20–24.

particularly a very important petrochemical project that was agreed to be implemented between the two countries in late 1979 before coming on stream successfully in early 1983.[1] The Taiwanese–Saudi Arabian technological cooperation, nevertheless, had not begun during the course of the first oil boom; nor did this area of bilateral cooperation come to an end in the aftermath of that agreeable era. The ROC, for instance, had agreed in the 1960s to give some help to Saudi Arabia in the field of agriculture before extending its assistances to other areas in the following decades.[2] When the Saudis ended their official diplomatic ties with Taipei in the early 1990s, the issue of technological assistance became even more delicate between the two countries. In order to curry favor with the Saudis in critical energy and commercial areas, the Taiwanese were willing to provide the Arab kingdom with some technological products and engineering services which the Saudis could not probably get easily or cheaply from other sources.[3] Over the past several decades, therefore, the ROC's technological connections to Saudi Arabia have covered different fields; from agricultural and fishing programs to medical and marketing training.[4]

Beyond Saudi Arabia, Taiwan engaged in considerable technological collaborations with many other countries throughout the Middle East, including Jordan, Bahrain, Qatar, Oman, the UAE, Israel, and Iran. The smaller countries in the region were particularly interested in the Taiwanese expertise and technologies in the field of renewable energies which have recently captured the attention of many people both in the public and private sectors.[5] Some countries were attracted to the ROC's technical

---

1 "The Industrial Cooperation between the ROC and the Arabian States," *Sino–Arabian Association Bulletin*, No. 47 (1983), p. 49.

2 Office of Technology Assessment, *Technology Transfer to the Middle East*, Publication no. OTA-ISC-173 (Washington, D.C.: Office of Technology Assessment, U.S. Government Printing Office, 1984), p. 343.

3 Andrew S. Cooper, *The Oil Kings: How the U.S., Iran, and Saudi Arabia Changed the Balance of Power in the Middle East* (New York: Simon & Schuster Paperbacks, 2011), p. 160.

4 "Taiwanese Products Impress Saudi Traders," *Saudi Gazette*, June 14, 2014.

5 "Focus on Taiwan: Saudi–Taiwanese Ties Grow as New Avenues Open," *Arab News*, October 19, 2010; and "Taiwan and the Gulf: The Sky's the Limit?" *Middle East Institute*, July 18, 2012.

know-how in the area of managing water resources productive-
ly, while others were intrigued by the Taiwanese technique to
save more energy in apartments and other living spaces.[1] There
were still larger countries in the region besides Saudi Arabia
which could provide good opportunities for some Taiwanese
companies to engage in more sophisticated and bigger bilateral
projects.[2] A case in point is Iran which signed a number of auto
deals with the East Asian country in order to jointly produce
environmental-friendly yet affordable cars and personal vehicles
for its insatiable domestic markets.[3]

Deep down, there happened to be two major characteristics
in Taiwan's overall pattern of technological collaborations with
the Middle Eastern countries over the past several decades. First,
the Taiwanese from either the public or private sectors were not
willing to generously share with the region all their newfangled
technologies and highly-advanced materials. Such a conservative approach had a lot to do with the way the Taiwanese themselves had struggled for decades to acquire, from every possible
source, the technology and scientific know-how they deemed
necessary for their own development and industrialization programs.[4] Second, the ROC was not really in favor of taking advantage of its technical strength and high-tech capabilities as a
bargaining chip to get significant concessions *vis-à-vis* its Middle
Eastern partners no matter if such a cunning stratagem could
sometimes serve well to further the interests of Taiwan's active
Western and Eastern rivals in the region.[5] Such benign habit had

1 "Connected to the Middle East," *Taiwan Today*, February 1, 2014;
"Taiwan, Israel Seek Further Cooperation on Water Technology,"
Focus Taiwan, November 28, 2014; and "Taiwan Offers Smart Energy-
efficiency Solution for Buildings in Middle East," *Kuwait Times*, October
2, 2017.
2 "Taiwanese Developer Reveals Maryah Plaza Project," *Arabian Business*,
September 16, 2014.
3 "Taiwan's Luxgen Motor Co. to Enter Iran," *Financial Tribune*, July 16,
2017.
4 Douglas B. Fuller, "Taiwan's Industrial Policies for High-technology
Sectors 1975–2012," in Douglas B. Fuller and Murray A. Rubinstein,
eds., *Technology Transfer between the US, China and Taiwan: Moving Knowledge*
(Abingdon and New York: Routledge, 2013), pp. 47–70.
5 "UAE, Taiwan Trade Expected to Reach Dh26.4bn this Year," *Zawya*,
September 25, 2014; and "Taiwan Shines in Invention Fairs in Hong
Kong, Kuwait," *Focus Taiwan*, December 6, 2014.

again something to do with the ROC's politico-diplomatic deficit and drawback for which its technological advantages were
supposed to function as a boon and not as a liability.

More Subtle Means: Military Connections

The ROC's technological links to the Middle East were not
constrained only to ordinary and civilian sections. The island
East Asian country could also engage the region in some other
sensitive and strategic areas such as arms deals. Of course, Taiwan itself has long been a main consumer and importer of defense items and military equipment. From the very beginning,
however, Taiwan's special circumstances as well as frequently
changing international environment often played a major role in
convincing Taipei to overtime invest significantly in developing
its own indigenous capabilities in defense and military realms.[1]
This was particularly the case when Taiwan underwent considerable international arms restrictions and embargoes as more
and more friendly developed and advanced countries of high-
tech weaponry switched their diplomatic allegiance to Beijing
at the cost of Taipei. The ROC's preoccupations with cultivating its own internal military competence gradually paid off, en-
abling Taipei to thereby become a player in the murky market of
international armaments.[2] Its arms customers included, but not
limited to, Indonesia, the Philippines, a number of Latin American countries, and the Middle East.[3]

Taiwan's forays into the arms bazaar of the Middle East began most probably after the outbreak of the Iran–Iraq War in
1980. The ROC found out of the blue a unique opportunity to
engage in military deals with Iran largely because of Tehran's
dire troubles in accessing its erstwhile rich arms markets in the
West.[4] Like the ROK, Taiwan was producing American weap-

---

1 Michael T. Klare, *American Arms Supermarket* (Austin: University of
Texas Press, 1984), p. 175.
2 Taiwan even considered developing its own nuclear program, but the
idea was not endorsed by the American leaders. Engel, p. 210.
3 "Troubled Taiwan Shipping Line Cuts Iran Service," *Financial Tribune*,
April 23, 2017.
4 "Israel Draws the Line at Taiwan Deepening Ties with Iran – Envoy,"
BBC, July 25, 2010; and "Taiwan not to Curb Pursuit Trade Ties with
Iran," *Central News Agency*, July 27, 2010.

ons under license, and some of its military products could be useful to the Iranians, who were already in hell-for-leather pursuit of new military equipment or replacement parts for their artillery and ammunition, which had become hard to acquire due to the arms embargo imposed by the United States and other major Western European countries.[1] It is yet unknown to what extent Taipei eventually sold arms to Tehran covertly, and whether its clandestine weapons supply to Iran involved any intermediary or private dealer.[2] The same can also be said about Taiwan's probable arms deals with Iraq over the course of the Iran–Iraq War. After all, Taiwan was the only Northeast Asian state whose commercial vessels in the Persian Gulf waterway escaped the eight-year-long conflict unscathed, whereas ships belonging to its neighbors (including China, Japan, South Korea, and North Korea) all more or less were damaged or destroyed at some point during those dreadful and bloody years.[3]

Moreover, Israel turned out to be another critical arms partner of Taiwan in the Middle East region. Still, a great deal of the bilateral interactions between the two countries in defense and military areas was clandestine and devoid of media scrutiny, though their relations in many other fields were carefully kept on the hush-hush. On top of that, the nature and scope of the Taipei–Tel Aviv connections in almost all areas had a lot to do with their special relationship with the United States, and that is why Taiwan's ties with Israel, whether overt or covert, hardly followed a similar pattern widely seen in the ROC's interactions with many other countries in the Middle East both before and after the end of the Cold War era.[4] Besides sharing, rather discretely, their defense and military technologies and experiences, the ROC and the Jewish state often depended on Washington

---

1 Stockholm International Peace Research Institute (SIPRI), *The Arms Trade with the Third World* (New York: Holmes & Meier Publishers, 1975), p. 151.
2 Michael Brzoska, "Profiteering on the Iran–Iraq War," *Bulletin of the Atomic Scientists,* (June 1987), pp. 42–45.
3 Martin S. Navias and E. R. Hooton, *Tanker Wars: The Assault on Merchant Shipping during the Iran–Iraq Conflict, 1980–1988* (London and New York: I.B. Tauris, 1996), pp. 205–207.
4 Michael P. Ryan, *Playing By the Rules: American Trade Power and Diplomacy in the Pacific* (Washington, D.C.: Georgetown University Press, 1995), p. 51.

for the bulk of their cutting-edge subsystems and manufacturing techniques in order to keep up with the production of arms and munitions.

Despite their taste for certain weapons and military parts, however, the Arab countries of the Middle East could also cool Taiwan's desire to locate new customers for its arms exports. This external quest for new arms clients coincided with Taipei's own internal defense policy to diversify its main sources of weapons suppliers at a critical time when communist China's expanding military modernization continued to worry many concerned politicians and generals in the ROC.[1] In the post-Cold War period, therefor, one Taiwanese strategy to peddle some of its surplus military products was to lobby a number of willing and well-to-do Arab countries in the Middle East which had long fascinated many sophisticated arms manufacturers of the West because of their mindless spending spree on armaments. The ROC was prepared to even dispatch to the region surreptitiously its defense minister aiming to persuade the Arabs into more arms deals and military exchanges with Taipei no matter if the two sides did not enjoy normal politico-diplomatic relationship.[2]

Meanwhile, certain aspects of Taiwan's non-military relations with some Middle Eastern countries could still be regarded as a sort of transferring military technology to the region even when the island country had not initially engaged in a bilateral business for such purpose.[3] A case in point is the Taipei–Tehran commercial dealings some of which turned out to be highly controversial during the intractable presidency of Ahmadinejad.[4] A series of Western intelligence cables such as *WikiLeaks* and me-

---

1 William D. Hartung, "U.S.–Korea Jet Deal Boosts Arms Trade," *Bulletin of the Atomic Scientists*, Vol. 46, No. 9 (1990), pp. 18–24.
2 Geldenhuys, *Isolated States*, p. 486.
3 "Iran's Nuclear Smugglers 'Building a New Network in Taiwan'," *The Daily Telegraph*, December 11, 2009, p. 22; and "Taiwan dangju fouren tai shang shou yilang hewu yiqi weifan guiding" [Taiwan Authorities Deny Selling Iran Nuclear Equipment in Violation of Legal Provisions], *Huanghe xinwen wang* [Yellow News Network], March 9, 2010.
4 "Bureau Clarifies Report on Company Selling Nuclear Components to Iran," *Central News Agency*, December 18, 2009; "Yi taiwanren shexian cong meiguo xiang yilang zousi daodan lingjian beibu" [A Taiwanese Man Suspected of Smuggling U.S. Missile Parts to Iran Arrested], *Zhongguo guoji guangbo* [China Radio International], February 5, 2010;

dia outlets like the German *Der Spiegel* reported that a number of Taiwanese companies had shipped to Iran, either directly or through intermediaries, equipment and parts some of which were suspected to have dual-use civilian and military capabilities.[1] The Persian Gulf country was already under sever international sanctions because of its controversial nuclear program, and many in the West worried that Tehran could appropriately take advantage of those Taiwanese technologies germane to its missile and nuclear designs even when those equipment and parts had originally been purchased and shipped from the United States by a Taiwanese businessman or businesswoman.[2]

For their part, the authorities in Taiwan often promptly denied every time their country's direct or intermediary role in transferring sensitive technological equipment and technical know-how which the Iranians could exploit in any way for their controversial missile and nuclear programs. They also promised to cooperate duly with any third-party stakeholder (normally the United States) in putting a solid stop to the involvement of private Taiwanese nationals as well as those with Taiwanese dual citizenship who were willing to collaborate with Iran in return for huge financial rewards promised by Tehran.[3] Unlike the Iran–Iraq War period, moreover, modern technologies and sophisticated detective equipment had already made it very difficult for the ROC and its major companies to easily and freely engage in sensitive and suspicious Iran-related businesses inimical to the vital interests of Taipei's close allies and partners in the West and the Middle East, though there still happened to be some ambitious and recalcitrant Taiwanese nationals who had

---

and "Taiwan Man Tried to Export Missile Parts to Iran," *The China Post*, May 15, 2010.

1 "Xifang chaozuo yilang jiejin Taiwan" [The West's Speculations about Iran's Rapprochement with Taiwan], *Shijie xinwen bao* [World News Journal], March 14, 2008; "Iran Seeks Nuclear Parts through Taiwan," *The Telegraph*, December 10, 2009; and "US Worried over Taiwan's Exports to Iran: WikiLeaks," *Taipei Times*, Jun 12, 2011, p. 3.

2 "Hong Kong, Taiwan and Mainland Middlemen Help Iran Obtain Banned Components," *South China Morning Post*, November 20, 2012.

3 "Taiwanese Jailed in US for Illegal Exports to Iran," *Taipei Times*, October 26, 2012, p. 1.

the guts to risk their professional business and personal comfort in exchange for lucrative yet furtive deals with Iran.[1]

Belated Capitalizing on Culture

In comparison to commercial connections, cultural interactions have by and large received less attention and investment in the ROC's overall approach toward the Middle East. This is probably no coincidence as the two regions share few cultural commonalities where it comes to the dominant linguistic and cultural characteristics with which they affiliate.[2] For more than half a century, there happened to be little genuine people to people interactions other than those occasions when a state-sponsored program or ceremony could temporarily bring groups of public employees or private citizens together. And despite an increasingly growing economic interests of the ROC in the Middle East, successive governments in Taipei did little, if any, to instill into the minds of their citizens some passion and enthusiasm for the region. Such apathy was in sharp contrast to the government's staunch promotion of cultural tie-in between Taiwan and a selected number of regions and countries with which the Taiwanese people were widely encouraged to develop friendship, relationship, and even kinship.[3]

What particularly epitomizes the foregoing inertia and impassivity is a rather poor situation of Middle East studies in Taiwan. Out of its rather large community of public and private educational institutions and research centers throughout the island, only one Taiwanese academic body, National Chengchi University, was given the mandate to launch Arabic and Turkish languages programs in order to cater to practical needs of the country's policy and business circles. The state, and gener-

1 "U.S. Charges Taiwan Citizen over Iran Exports," *Reuters*, February 4, 2010; "Illegal Exports to Iran on the Rise, Say U.S. Officials," *Los Angeles Times*, November 17, 2012; and "Taiwan Man Admits Sending Exports to Iran from Texas," *San Antonio Express*, June 25, 2015.
2 Georg Woodman, *Cultural Shock-Taiwan: Cow Mentality, Rubber Slipper Fashion in BinLang Country* (Philadelphia, PA: Xlibris Corporation, 2010), p. 97.
3 "Taiwan's Donations to Middle East Refugees Top US$7 Million," *The China Post*, October 6, 2014; and "Taiwan to Donate Temporary Housing to Refugees in Iraq," *Taipei Times*, December 10, 2014, p. 3.

ally the public sector, in Taiwan paid very little attention to this matter even after the oil shocks of the early and late 1970s, while both the Japanese and South Korean governments considerably invested in Middle Eastern research and academic programs in the aftermath of those cataclysmic politico-economic developments which shell-shocked almost all heavily energy-dependent consumers throughout the world. That is why Japan and the ROK now have an upper hand where it comes to education, research, and publication about the Middle East, though both countries feel they are still far behind their counterparts in the West.[1]

The situation was not much better in the realm of religion.[2] For instance, the building of the Taipei Grand Mosque in 1960 was made possible by generous funding and donations provided by the king of Jordan and the Shah of Iran during the heydays of their bilateral relationship with the Chinese nationalists now ruling the rust in Taipei. Probably the only difference was that the ROC had been able to use somehow effectively the potentials of its Muslim minority to smooth the way for different types of politico-diplomatic as well as economic connections to the Middle East.[3] Currently numbered around 20,000 people, the Taiwanese Muslims were somewhat instrumental in either initiating or improving the ROC's relationship with some Mideast countries, the Arab ones in particular.[4] Influential members of the Muslim community of Taiwan could greatly assist their country to curry favor with the Saudi officials as the annual pilgrimage of this religious group to the Arab country had a lot of

1 James H. Grayson, *Korea: A Religious History* (New York: RoutledgeCurzon, 2002), p. 196.
2 The ROC, nonetheless, had fostered rather good connections to the Muslim Uighur minority of the mainland China by hosting the exiled Xinjiang government. For more details on this topic, for instance, see: Justin M. Jacobs, *Xinjiang and the Modern Chinese State* (Seattle: University of Washington Press, 2016).
3 "Taiwan Tourism Looks to Raise Awareness in Middle East," *Travel Daily Media*, June 15, 2016; "Taiwan Becomes Preferred Destination for the Middle East Traveller in 2017," *Emirates 24/7*, May 22, 2017; and "Taiwan Woos Southeast Asia, Middle East Travellers with Muslim-friendly Food," *Channel News Asia*, June 25, 2017.
4 "Taiwan's Relations with Saudi Arabia: An Interview with Ibrahim Chao," *Middle East Institute*, December 8, 2014; and "Islam in Taiwan: Lost in Tradition," *Al Jazeera*, December 31, 2014.

benefits in facilitating Taipei's cultural diplomacy toward the Saudis and some other nations in the region.[1]

To counterbalance its historically lethargic attitudes toward the cultural issues of the ROC–Middle East nexus, nevertheless, Taiwan has shown a keen desire in recent years to make the most of culture while dealing with the region. The Taiwanese public and especially the private sectors seem to have become more cognizant of the importance of cultural potentials in forging closer and long-term connections to the Middle East countries.[2] From carving out some educational and scholarship programs to launching recreational and sports exchanges, the ROC has particularly focused on younger generation to further its newly-designed cultural objectives toward the region, though not all countries in the Middle East have received equal attention from such cultural agenda.[3] Moreover, Taiwan like some of its rivals in East Asia has recently made a serious effort to adjust its society to an increasing number of Middle Eastern tourists many of whom seem to have found the island country a more conducive environment to their own cultural traditions and personal taste.[4]

Reciprocal interest was a boon. A surprising hike in the number of tourists, students, and business travelers, for instance, motivated the Emirates to launch the first direct flight between Dubai and Taipei in February 2014.[5] In the same way, the national flag carrier of Turkey, the Turkish Airlines, brought into being its direct flight between the two countries in March

1 "Sino-Iranian Association Inaugurated," *Taiwan Review*, July 5, 1970.
2 "Taiwan to Donate 100,000 US Dollars for Iran Quake Relief," *BBC*, December 27, 2003; "Iran Ready to Send Humanitarian Aids to Taiwan," *Asia News Monitor*, August 20, 2009; and "Taiwan Volunteers Prepare Clothes for Syrian Refugees," *Tzu Chi Foundation*, October 18, 2012.
3 "Taiwan, Israel to Advance Education, Youth, Sports Exchanges," *Focus Taiwan*, December 3, 2014; "Taiwan Turns up Charm to Woo Muslim Travellers," *The Straits Times*, July 25, 2016; and "Taiwan Builds Bridge with Israel through Arts and Culture," *i24 News*, September 6, 2016.
4 "Taiwan Extends Medical Reach to UAE," *Taipei Times*, May 14, 2014, p. 4; "Taiwan Keen to Lure Middle East Travelers," *Travel Daily Media*, January 15, 2014; and "Taiwan Considered a Top Destination for Muslims," *The China Post*, March 19, 2015.
5 "Taiwan Upbeat about Direct Flight Accord with Turkey," *The China Post*, December 26, 2014.

2015, giving many interested Taiwanese people a chance to take advantage of the Middle East country's favorable location as a transit point to the neighboring regions.[1] Such developments could also help give some publicity to Taiwan, which was rather unknown in the wider Middle East.[2] After all, an unprecedented groundswell of interest among Mideast elites in recent success-ful models of economic growth and social modernization, par-ticularly the East Asian model, could contribute significantly to the ROC's soft power profile and smooth the way for its cultural demarches throughout the region.[3]

Conclusion

The contemporary history of Taiwan's relationship with the Middle East can be divided into three distinctive periods. In the first period which lasted from 1949 until the early 1970s, Taiwan experienced the acme of its amicable bilateral relations with many powerful and influential Middle Eastern countries. The pressure-cooking politics of Taiwan had propitiously managed to establish a raft of favorable links to the topsy-turvy world of the Middle East, providing an appropriate ground for Taipei to gradually lay down some basic foundations of a multifaceted relationship with the region. The ROC enjoyed a high level of politico-diplomatic recognition as well as growing commercial connections to the region. The East Asian island country was equally in good terms with many small to medium-sized Mid-east states whose timely sympathy and solidarity were critically important for Taipei's tottering legal international status and authority.

1 "Taiwan Opens Arms for Muslim Travelers," *Arabian Gazette*, February 20, 2016; "Taiwan Woos Muslim Tourists," *Daily Express*, May 14, 2017; and "Emirates Says Telling Cabin Crew not to Wear Taiwan Flag Pins per China's Request was an 'Error'," *South China Morning Post*, May 31, 2017.

2 "Taiwan Eases Visa Regulations for Iran, Iraq Businessmen," *Central News Agency*, July 19, 2009; "Taiwan–Turkey Business Council to be Held in May," *The China Post*, May 2, 2014; and "Taiwan and Turkey Sign Reciprocal Free E-visas Agreement to Boost Tourism," *The China Post*, February 3, 2016.

3 "Taiwan Touts its Attractions at UAE Arabian Travel Mart," *The China Post*, May 6, 2014; "Taiwan–Israel Youth Program Ends 7-day Tour," *The China Post*, May 31, 2014; and "Taiwan Academician Wins Khwarizmi Award," *Taiwan Today*, February 12, 2015.

During the second period, whose time span started in early 1970s and ended in early 1990s, Taiwan had to ineluctably struggle with its tough luck in the Middle East, though what it experienced in the region then was simply an extension of what the ROC had been cold-bloodedly forced to bear with on a larger world stage. Almost all friendly Middle East countries switched their diplomatic allegiance from the ROC to communist China, leaving Taipei to maintain normal politico-diplomatic relations with Saudi Arabia alone. As the last remaining relic of normalcy, therefore, Taiwan's bilateral relationship with the Saudis in the Middle East translated into one of the most pivotal state-to-state bonds throughout the 1970s and 1980s. Moreover, the ROC's economic interests in the region grew by leaps and bounds, though the significance of hard politics was alwys at the fore because Taiwan's priorities were now mostly about keeping its breakneck economic growth and industrialization on track while staying alert to any threats to its political survival and economic success in the long run.

Finally, the third period covers the post-1991 era during which the ROC has seen the pinnacle of its anomalous relationship with the Middle East. It has been stripped of any type of normal politico-diplomatic relations with any Middle Eastern country amid increasingly expanding commercial connections to the region. Friendly and close political ties with Mideast nations have been off the table, but that annoying impediment has not really stopped Taipei from approaching many of those countries for bilateral interactions in areas including economic, technological, cultural, and even low-keyed military cooperation. Additionally, the ROC seems to have learned to be content with the nature and scope of its present relationship with the Middle East in the hope that the achievements in non-political areas will tip the balance. After all, it is not really an easy matter to score big in many non-politico-diplomatic realms without playing kissy-face politics in one of the most politicized regions in the world.

CHAPTER 6. DOLLAR DANCES WITH DIRHAM: HONG KONG'S
GROWING MIDEAST ROLE

Of all East Asia, Hong Kong's connection to the Middle East has probably received the least scholarly attention across the globe. Academic studies on that topic are almost non-existent, while non-academic works are sparse and scattered. Moreover, the Hong Kong element is also ignored in many fields where research projects have concentrated on China's relationship with the Middle East. The same shortcoming still exists in other studies which broadly tackle an issue in East Asia's links to the Mideast region. If there had been some justification for such disregard when Hong Kong was not under Chinese rule, it made little sense to ignore the unique role of Hong Kong, either alone or as an integral part of China, in the expanding nexus of East Asian–Middle Eastern relations.

Given China's ever-expanding multifaceted interests throughout the Middle East over the past decades, how did then Hong Kong serve Beijing to put into practice some of its commercial and non-economic policies in the region? And since the geographic location, modern politico-economic history, and governance of Hong Kong are somewhat contrasting as compared to some other major Chinese cities, which parts of the Middle East were particularly more conducive to their growing bilateral interactions? More importantly, has the gradual "Chinization" of

Hong Kong over the past two decades influence markedly the nature and scope of its various connections to the Middle East?

Peculiar connections: Dollar dances with Dirham

In spite of all hindrances adumbrated above, Hong Kong has surprisingly played a very important role in the East Asian, and especially Chinese, connections to the Middle East in commercial, and even politico-cultural, areas favorable to the two regions. Officially known as the Hong Kong Special Administrative Region (SAR) of the PRC, this relatively autonomous territory has sometimes been instrumental in such cross-regional interactions particularly since the time it was handed over, or actually returned, to the Chinese in July 1997.[1] Because of its unique characteristics, Hong Kong has been more relevant to the economic and financial aspects of the East Asia–Middle East dynamics over the past several decades. But even this dominant pecuniary area has sometimes required the SAR to take advantage of its other potentials to either initiate or facilitate the pure commercial interactions involving the two regions.[2] As measured by the frequent meetings and negotiations between top officials of the SAR and their Middle Eastern counterparts, it seems that Hong Kong's relationship with the region has become many-faceted, covering politico-economic, financial, technological, and cultural tie-ups.

Still, a sketch of Hong Kong's overall interactions with the Middle East shows that three issues deserve particular attention. One issue is about Hong Kong's location as a major trade entrepôt which has greatly contributed to the SAR's increasing exchanges with Middle Eastern states and especially with those similar port cities in the region. As a matter of fact, a great deal of Hong Kong's myriad connections to and relative success in the Middle East region boils down to this distinctive characteristic.

1 Jeffrey Henderson, *East Asian Transformation: On the Political Economy of Dynamism, Governance and Crisis* (Abingdon and New York: Routledge, 2011), pp. 68–69.
2 Christopher A. McNally, "Reflections on Capitalism and China's Emergent Political Economy," in Christopher A. McNally, ed., *China's Emergent Political Economy: Capitalism in the Dragon's Lair* (Abingdon and New York: Routledge, 2008), pp. 17–36.

A second issue is about Hong Kong's often controversial and sometimes subterranean relationship with Iran in more recent decades. Although the SAR's entrepôt capacity has again been a major factor behind its growing links to Iran, nonetheless, Hong Kong's modern connections to other parts of the Middle East region have by and large been devoid of such contentious matters involving the SAR and the Persian Gulf country.[1] Finally, the third issue deals with non-commercial interactions other than those initiated or sponsored by the formal and public sectors. This aspect of the Hong Kong–Middle East relationship is largely cultural in nature, and its realization may not be necessarily and predominantly attributed to the entrepôt factor.

Ace in the hole: The efficacy of a trade entrepôt

In the lexicon of international trade, an entrepôt normally refers to a commercial hub where goods are imported in order to be re-exported sometimes by using different modes of transportation. Whether or not the re-exported commodities are repackaged in an entrepôt, they are certainly sold at a higher rate. After all, an entrepôt can survive and thrive on such a mark-up because it conventionally does not impose high customs duties on the goods enter there from a source territory. An entrepôt is, therefore, associated with a trading center where merchandise can be re-distributed to other places, no matter how far or close, without adding outrageous import duties on the goods which are originally imported to that commercial midpoint.[2] By playing such a facilitating and constructive role, an entrepôt oils the wheels of indirect trade between different regions and territories, though it may also produce some other important results such as job creation. That is why this pattern of international commerce has considerably played an indispensable role in the

---

1 "Hong Kong Works to Keep Islamic Finance Momentum as Firms Balk," *Reuters*, December 10, 2014; "Why Hong Kong is the New Saudi Arabia," *Forbes*, January 8, 2016; and "Saudi Aramco Shortlists Hong Kong, London and New York for IPO," *Middle East Economic Digest* (MEED), January 14, 2018.
2 Peter J. Buckley, *Studies in International Business* (New York: St. Martin's Press, 1992), p. 39–40.

rise and ascendency of Hong Kong in East Asia and Dubai in the Middle East.[1]

Hong Kong has had a relatively long history of functioning as an entrepôt by serving commercial interests of various lands and territories. Because of encountering with modern patterns of international trade somewhat on a daily basis, this function was particularly developed during the period when Hong Kong was a British colony from 1841 until June 1997.[2] Hong Kong's entrepôt role underwent further developments after its sovereignty was transferred to the communist China which itself was unprecedentedly experiencing enormous changes in its commercial interactions with the outside world.

As the Chinese mercantile turnover with other regions ratcheted up by leaps and bounds, Hong Kong turned out to become a much more pivotal commercial midpoint through linking the mainland businesses to different parts of the world.[3] Besides its convenient geographical location, the SAR enjoyed certain other advantages which few, if any, other Chinese port cities could offer, including free trade, open markets, minimal customs duties, etc.[4] As far as the East Asian, and especially Chinese, trade with the Middle East was concerned, these appealing attributes would better smooth the way for bilateral and multilateral commercial interactions if Hong Kong could pair up with similar places in the Mideast region.

In the Middle East, Dubai is probably the only port city which comes close to Hong Kong in terms of entrepôt trade.[5] Unlike

---

1 "A Mexican Restaurant from Hong Kong in Dubai?" *Gulf News*, May 9, 2016; "Emirates Resumes Flights to Hong Kong," *Gulf News*, August 24, 2017; "Saudi King Salman Receives Hong Kong Leader Carrie Lam," *Al-Arabiya*, December 3, 2017; and "M&S Sells Hong Kong Business to Franchise Partner," *Financial Times*, January 2, 2018.
2 Lawrence Mills, *Protecting Free Trade: The Hong Kong Paradox 1947–1997* (Hong Kong: Hong Kong University Press, 2012), p. 1.
3 Gordon Mathews, *Ghetto at the Center of the World: Chungking Mansions, Hong Kong* (Chicago and London: The University of Chicago Press, 2011), p. 1.
4 Rolf D. Cremer, and Mary J. Willes, *The Tongue of the Tiger: Overcoming Language Barriers in International Trade* (Singapore: World Scientific Publishing Co., 1998), pp. 29–31.
5 "Sharjah Firm Welcomes Hong Kong Investment Opportunities," *Al Bawaba*, September 4, 2014; "Hong Kong Sees Trade with Sultanate Growing over 10 Times in Next 5 Years," *Zawya*, November 16, 2014; and

the SAR, however, Dubai has a rather modest historical record in this area as a great deal of its modern success and cachet is sensibly attributed to an ill-gotten fate sadly befallen upon many other more resourceful and convenient locations in the Persian Gulf and the rest of the greater Middle East region.[1] Blessed by a whole host of supportive external and internal inducements, Dubai has thereby managed to unexpectedly position itself as a leading entrepôt in the entire Mideast region, though the Arab port city has equally been successful in a number of other economic and non-economic spheres as well.[2] Today, a lion's share of the United Arab Emirates' non-energy exports and imports are practically handled through Dubai, making the port city the richest and most important place in the Arab Sheikhdom.[3] More important, Dubai's entrepôt function has significantly boosted its status as a major commercial midpoint between the Middle East and other parts of the world, including Hong Kong in East Asia.[4]

True that the East Asian states such as China did not necessarily need Dubai to engage in commercial interactions with their partners across the Middle East. But such argument makes sense only when things in the Mideast region work under normal circumstances. The problem is that at least since the outbreak of the Iran–Iraq War in 1980, the Middle East, particularly

"Bahrain Aims to be Hong Kong to Saudi Arabia's China," *Arab News,* January 27, 2018.

1 Peter Lilley, *Dirty Dealing: The Untold Truth about Global Money Laundering, International Crime and Terrorism* (London and Philadelphia: Kogan Page, 2006), p. 149.

2 International Monetary Fund, *United Arab Emirates: Selected Issues and Statistical Appendix* (Washington, D.C.: International Monetary Fund, 2003), p. 6.

3 Raymond Barrett, *Dubai Dreams: Inside the Kingdom of Bling* (London and Boston: Nicholas Brealey, 2010); and International Monetary Fund, *United Arab Emirates: 2002 Article IV Consultation-Staff Country Reports* (Washington, D.C.: International Monetary Fund, 2003), p. 4.

4 Surprisingly, Hong Kong and Dubai share in common many critical characteristics, both in positive and negative ways; from hosting impressive skyscrapers and glittering offices of international finance firms to providing a fertile ground for prostitution and modern slavery. "Dubai in United Arab Emirates a Centre of Human Trafficking and Prostitution," *Sydney Morning Herald,* January 21, 2016; "Hong Kong One of Asia's Worst Countries for Slavery, Despite City's Wealth," *CNBC,* October 31, 2016; and "Dubai to Hong Kong, Follow the Money (Laundering)," *South China Morning Post,* August 5, 2018.

the Persian Gulf region, has been in the throes of military conflict and various forms of economic turbulence.[1] These perpetual
anomalous conditions left Iraq, and especially Iran, to muddle
through at the whim of neighboring ports like Dubai.[2] Of course,
this was not a one-sided problem because partners such as East
Asian countries sorely needed to take advantage of a number of
accessible and convenient entrepôts like Hong Kong and Dubai
in order to handle their lucrative commercial interactions with
Iran, which has long been in a penalty box by sundry international sanctions.[3] The stakes were simply too high, and that is
a reason why sometimes such bilateral and multilateral dealings could end up becoming contentious, scandalous, or just
inconceivable.

Going subterranean: Hong Kong–Iran connections make international headlines

Hong Kong has certainly played a very crucial role in Iran's
international trade with the East Asian countries, China in
particular. The PRC is Iran's top trading partner, and the SAR
has ineluctably been instrumental in the Sino–Iranian commercial interactions through transshipment, entrepôt trade,
and direct trade. Interestingly, a hike in the scope and size of
Iran's economic relationship with China started to gain momentum soon after Hong Kong came under a full control of
the Chinese. Moreover, the top officials in Hong Kong have
increasingly become cognizant of the SAR's distinctive position in the growing pace of the Sino–Iranian connections over
the past several years. As Iran and China have vowed about

1 "Hong Kong's Role in Kidnapping of Libyan Dissident Sami alSaadi
Back in Spotlight," *South China Morning Post*, December 13, 2014.
2 "Dubai Traders Call for Relief on Iran Exports," *The National*, January 3,
2012; "UAE to Boost Trade Ties with Hong Kong: Saleh," *Khaleej Times*,
December 12, 2013; and "Hong Kong Keen to Use Dubai as Gateway to
Mena," *Khaleej Times*, November 10, 2014.
3 "Qatar Buys $1bn Stake in Hong Kong Energy Trust from Li Kashing,"
Financial Times, June 9, 2015; "Hong Kong Teams Up with Dubai to
Promote Fintech Innovation," *South China Morning Post*, August 28, 2017;
"Dubai Exports Agency Opens Trade Office in Hong Kong," *Arabian
Business*, September 5, 2017; "Hong Kong Leader Carrie Lam Talks Up
Saudi Arabia as Trade Partner in 'Belt and Road' Push," *South China
Morning Post*, December 5, 2017; and "UAE Imports from Hong Kong
Reaches $13.2bln," *Zawya*, December 20, 2017.

the prospect of a $600 billion turnover in bilateral commercial ties between Tehran and Beijing, Hong Kong seems to be further preoccupied with the thought of how to make most of such eventuality by playing the card of its strategic location wisely.[1] But a major impediment to this aromatic anticipation is whether the two sides can fully overcome rumors and controversies related to their connections which often ruffled the feathers of other stakeholders over the past decades.

Disputatious claims with regard to certain aspects of Iran's commercial connections to Hong Kong go back to the time when the critical port city was still under British rule. In the period between 1984 and 1997, the Executive Council in Hong Kong closed down several companies which accused of illegal interactions with Iran. In 1995 alone, for instance, Hong Kong shut down seven companies which had reportedly engaged in transferring banned products to the Persian Gulf country. Prominent among those entities was Rex International Development affiliated with the state-owned China North Industries (Norinco), which had been indicted for allegedly shipping "chemical weapons precursors" to Iran.[2] These companies were suspected of providing the Iranians with some sensitive technologies or delicate chemicals which could be exploited both in civilian and military sectors, but it is still hard to prove that whether and to what extent such dual-use goods were actually utilized for any illegal purpose.

Although no Hong Kongese company was closed down on such grounds after the port city returned to Chinese authority, the SAR's connections to Iran underwent tighter international scrutiny during the presidency of Ahmadinejad (August

---

1 "Iranian Trade Delegation to Visit Hong Kong This Week," *Tehran Times*, November 26, 2006; "Hong Kong Eyes Shipping Boost from China's New Silk Road, Iran," *Reuters*, June 10, 2016; "Hong Kong Eyes Closer Maritime Cooperation with Tehran," *Tasnim News Agency*, June 11, 2016; "Hong Kongese Business Delegation to Visit Iran Soon," *Tehran Times*, October 29, 2016; "Iran, Hong Kong Sign MOU on Economic Co-op," *Tehran Times*, November 9, 2016; and "Top Legislator Eyes Hong Kong's Role in Belt and Road Initiative," *Xinhua*, February 3, 2018.
2 For more information, see: "The Hong Kong Connection," *South China Morning Post*, February 27, 2011; and Roger Howard, *Iran in Crisis?: The Future of the Revolutionary Regime and the US Response* (London and New York: Zed Books Ltd, 2004), p. 103.

2005–August 2013).[1] Particularly from 2008 onward, a number of Western media outlets and journals published reports about the involvement of some companies and private citizens from Hong Kong, and a number of other East Asian countries, in the illegal transfer of nuclear components and other sensitive technologies to Iran which they claimed violated different sanction laws against Tehran.[2] Whenever such news broke out, the authorities in charge promptly denied the incident, promising to investigate the matter at hand as quick as possible through close cooperation with non-regional stakeholders.[3] Whether or not such claims were plausible in the first place and regardless of the willingness of those parties to take risks and engage in any "illegal" business, Hong Kong, like other East Asian states, was widely expected in the West to implement all the stipulated sanctions against Iran, and to stay away from any means that could potentially help Tehran circumvent those levied punishments.[4]

Meanwhile, Hong Kong had its own fair share of troubles with regard to the sanctions bills or their alleged violations by companies and private individuals. One problem was that the port city was not initially prepared, for whatever reason, to swiftly implement all the sanctions levied against Iran. It took the top officials in the SAR, for instance, some nine months to come up with measures regarding the implementation of one of the sanctions bills enacted by the United Nations in 2010.[5] Probably pressures wielded by Beijing behind the scene was a culprit behind such reluctance, because China was often accused by the West that it was not willing enough to comply with all the rules dictated by the sanctions simply for the huge economic interests the Chinese were enjoying in the wake of

---

1 "US Sanctions Hong Kong Shippers over Iran Trade," *AFP*, January 13, 2011.
2 "Hong Kong, Taiwan and Mainland Middlemen Help Iran Obtain Banned Components," *South China Morning Post*, November 20, 2012.
3 "Hong Kong Passes Laws to Seize Iran-linked Assets," *AFP*, March 30, 2011.
4 "Four Iranian Cargo Vessels to Quit Hong Kong Register," *South China Morning Post*, November 17, 2012.
5 "HK Enacts Iran Sanctions Law after 9 Months," *South China Morning Post*, March 30, 2011; and "HK Shell Firms Helping Iranian Shipper May Escape Penalty," *South China Morning Post*, April 5, 2011.

those international punishments pushed against the Iranians.[1] Another problem was that the SAR could hardly exercise total control over all the individuals and companies which were to engage in some potential illegal dealings with the Iranians. Not all of them possessed the nationality of Hong Kong, and there happened to be certain front companies and fraudulent individuals who were simply taking advantage of the SAR to smooth the way for their lucrative business with Iran.

Non-commercial links: Cultural and recreational allures

As a corollary to their contemporary developments and societal transformation, Hong Kong and many major cities across the Middle East have increasingly become a rendezvous for regional and international cultural events. Many such cultural occurrences are now jointly held between institutions and individual stakeholders from the SAR and the Mideast region. The public sector might still play a considerable role in initiating and implementing cultural events between the SAR and the Middle Eastern countries, but the private sector in both regions is also increasingly find itself at the forefront of such projects. The main focus has significantly diversified over the years, covering sports competitions, film and music festivals, museums and art galleries, catering and culinary festivities, literary and book exhibitions, etc.[2] Such cultural and educational events may last only for a short while, but long-lasting cultural trends between the two parties are increasingly becoming popular as well.

Education is probably one of the most pivotal contributors to the dynamics of the Hong Kong–Middle East relationship. Hong Kong has certainly a number of attractive educational and academic advantages which greatly appeal to Middle East citizens who choose East Asia to either build up their scholastic records or simply hone their scientific and technical skills

1 "Tehran Hosts 'Hong Kong, China's Trade Gateway' Confab," *Tehran Times*, December 22, 2008.
2 "Emirati Literature Gets Fans in Hong Kong," *Khaleej Times*, July 23, 2017; "Hong Kong UAV Sparkles in Iraq," *Aviation Week*, November 13, 2017; "Lebanon Goes Up 1-0 VS. Hong Kong in Asian Cup Qualifiers," *The Daily Star*, November 14, 2017; and "Dubai PR Agency Picks Up Key Wins at Hong Kong Event," *Gulf News*, December 12, 2017.

in different fields.[1] Besides offering the attractive benefit of the English language, the SAR provides a whole host of other socio-cultural comforts which a Middle Eastern national, with a thoroughly different mindset and culture, may not easily find in many other parts of East Asia. On the other side, a growing number of interested people from Hong Kong select a Middle Eastern country to pursue their higher education, many of them concentrating on a discipline in social studies and humanities. Of course, part of this trend stems from economic opportunities that the modern Middle East–Hong Kong connections have created.[2]

Another trend is that a growing number of people from Hong Kong and Middle Eastern countries choose the other side for their leisure and recreational activities.[3] The SAR and an increasing number of Middle Eastern cities are even becoming a destination for long-term expat life and retirement.[4] For many Middle East tourists and travelers, Hong Kong is an exotic option to either visit or for flight connections to other East Asian cities and Oceania.[5] With regard to the Hong Kongese, the Middle East is a giant swathe of territory which gives them many options to choose from.[6] The region is very diverse and relatively cheap, while its convenient location tempts visiting Hong Kongese to include in their itinerary a trip to the neigh-

1 Martin Hyde and Anthony Hyde, *Going to University Abroad: A Guide to Studying Outside the UK* (Abingdon and New York: Routledge, 2014).
2 Richard A. Clarke, *The Scorpion's Gate* (New York: The Penguin Putnam Inc., 2005); and "It is Time for Hong Kong's Youth to Explore a Career Path in the Middle East," *South China Morning Post*, January 15, 2018.
3 "New Wave of Iranian Globetrotters Hits the Road," *AFP*, January 31, 2018.
4 Interestingly, these places are also becoming an attractive choice for criminals, runaways, tax exiles, political exiles, etc. As a case in point, two former Thai Prime Ministers, Yingluck Shinawatra and her brother Thaksin Shinawatra, have settled in Dubai for their self-exiled life. See, "Ex-Thailand PM Yingluck Shinawatra Flees to Dubai amid Jail Threat," *Sky News*, August 26, 2017.
5 "Hong Kong Expects Surge in Tourists from Qatar," *Gulf Times*, May 24, 2014; "Martial Art Sets Hong Kong Iranian Immigrant on a Better Path," *South China Morning Post*, August 16, 2016; and "24 Hours in Hong Kong," *The National*, December 7, 2017.
6 "Sotheby's Hong Kong to Present Exhibition of Middle East Art in Asia," *Xinhua*, October 24, 2017; and "Saudi Arabia Grants Citizenship to Hong Kong Robot Sophia – with Rights Ahead of Real Women and Foreign Workers," *South China Morning Post*, October 30, 2017.

boring European or African region.[1] More and more airlines from the SAR and the Middle East are adding flights in order to cope with the demands and make certain that their rivals will not easily capture this rewarding market.[2]

Conclusion

Because of its critical geographic location and contemporary internal dynamics, Hong Kong has developed multi-pronged relations with the Middle East over the past several decades. The SAR has thereby become increasingly susceptible to any development which may take place across the region. The rise of the Islamic State, for instance, led to the securitization of certain matters in Hong Kong–Middle East interactions, though the SAR itself was also influenced by such a sensational occurrence.[3]

Still, to a great extent the modern relationship between Hong Kong and the Middle East has to do with three critical issues: the role and functions of a trade entrepôt, subtle and often illicit connections in commerce and finance, and varied forms of cultural and educational links. Although political and security matters may temporarily dominate Hong Kong's ties with the Middle East, however, economic and cultural elements are expected to firmly hold sway over a bulk of the Chinese SAR's ever-expanding interactions with the region for a foreseeable future. Even when the security and strategic interests of China in the Middle East become increasingly complex

1 "Why Travel to Iran Should be Next on Your Bucket List," *South China Morning Post*, June 2, 2017.
2 "Etihad and Hong Kong Airlines in Codeshare Deal," *The National*, December 17, 2014; "Dubai's Emirates to Launch Superjumbo Flights to Hong Kong," *South China Morning Post*, January 13, 2017; "Dubai Chosen as Cathay Pacific's Main Regional Hub," *The National*, September 4, 2017; "Qatar Airways to Take Stake in Hong Kong's Cathay Pacific," *Wall Street Journal*, November 5, 2017; and "Qatar Airways Raises Stake in Cathay Pacific Airways To 9.94%," *Nikkei Asian Review*, January 23, 2018.
3 "ISIS May Target Hong Kong for Recruitment Transit: Expert," *Want China Times*, April 6, 2015; "Hong Kong Police on Alert for Terror Threat from Lone Wolves Inspired by Islamic State," *South China Morning Post*, May 4, 2017; "Migrant Maids and Nannies for Jihad," *The New York Times*, July 18, 2017; and "What Turns a Hong Kong Maid towards Islamic State?" *South China Morning Post*, August 6, 2017.

and consequential, commercial benefits would most probably remain as the salient element of the SAR's growingly multifaceted relations with Middle East countries.

Bibliography

Abe, Shinzo. *Utsukushii kuni he* [Towards a Beautiful Country]. Tokyo: Bunshun Shinsho, 2006.

Albright, David. *Peddling Peril: How the Secret Nuclear Trade Arms America's Enemies*. New York: Free Press, 2010.

Alterman, Jon B., and John W. Garver. *The Vital Triangle: China, the United States, and the Middle East*. Washington, D.C.: Center for International and Strategic Studies, 2008.

Alton, David, and Rob Chidley. *Building Bridges: Is There Hope for North Korea?* Oxford: Lion Hudson, 2013.

Armstrong, Charles K. *Tyranny of the Weak: North Korea and the World, 1950–1992*. Ithaca and London: Cornell University Press, 2013.

Atkinson, Joel. "China–Taiwan Diplomatic Competition and the Pacific Islands." *The Pacific Review* 23, no. 4 (2010): 407–427.

Azad, Shirzad. "Japan's Gulf Policy and Response to the Iraq War." *Middle East Review of International Affairs* 12, no. 2 (2008): 52–64.

____. "Iran and the Two Koreas: A Peculiar Pattern of Foreign Policy." *The Journal of East Asian Affairs* 26, no. 2 (Fall/Winter 2012): 163–192.

____. "*Déjà vu* Diplomacy: South Korea's Middle East Policy under Lee Myung-bak." *Contemporary Arab Affairs* 6, no. 4 (2013): 552–566.

____. *Koreans in the Persian Gulf: Policies and International Relations*. Abingdon and New York: Routledge, 2015.

____. "Principlism Engages Pragmatism: Iran's Relations with East Asia under Ahmadinejad." *Asian Politics & Policy* 7, no. 4 (October 2015): 555–573.

____. *Iran and China: A New Approach to Their Bilateral Relations*. Lanham, MD: Lexington Books, 2017.

____. "Mutual Strategic Ambiguity: A Cautious Iranian–Chinese Approach to the Realization of the 'One Belt, One Road' Initiative." *International Symposium on China–Iran Cultural Communication and "One Belt, One Road Initiative": Conference Manual*. Beijing: Chinese Academy of Social Sciences (September 4–5, 2017): 102–108.

Bank of Korea. *Monthly Statistical Bulletin April 2011*. Seoul: BOK, 2011.

Barrett, Raymond. *Dubai Dreams: Inside the Kingdom of Bling*. London and Boston: Nicholas Brealey, 2010.

Beal, Tim. *North Korea: The Struggle against American Power*. London: Pluto Press, 2005.

Bechtol, Bruce E. *Red Rogue: The Persistent Challenge of North Korea*. Washington, D.C.: Potomac Books, 2007.

Bechtol, Bruce Jr. *The Last Days of Kim Jong-il: The North Korean Threat in a Changing Era*. Washington, D.C.: Potomac Books, 2013.

Behnke, Alison. *Kim Jong Il's North Korea*. Minneapolis, MN: Twenty-First Century Books, 2008.

Bell, Daniel A. *The China Model: Political Meritocracy and the Limits of Democracy*. Princeton, NJ: Princeton University Press, 2015.

Bennett, Bruce W. *Preparing for the Possibility of a North Korean Collapse*. Santa Monica, CA, and Washington, D.C.: Rand, 2013.

Bill, James A. *The Eagle and the Lion: The Tragedy of American–Iranian Relations*. New Haven and London: Yale University Press, 1988.

Bloodworth, Dennis, and Ching Ping Bloodworth. *The Chinese Machiavelli: 3000 Years of Chinese Statecraft*. New Brunswick and London: Transaction Publishers, 2009.

Blum, William. *Rogue State: A Guide to the World's Only Superpower*, third edition. London: Zed Books, 2006.

Brands, Hal. *From Berlin to Baghdad: America's Search for Purpose in the Post-Cold War World*. Lexington, KY: University Press of Kentucky, 2008.

Breen, Michael. *Kim Jong-il: North Korea's Dear Leader*. Hoboken, NJ: John Wiley, 2004.

Brown, Eugene. "Fire on the Other Side of the River: Japan and the Persian Gulf War." In *The Middle East after Iraq's Invasion of Kuwait*, edited by Robert O. Freedman. Gainesville, FL: University Press of Florida, 1993.

Brzoska, Michael. "Profiteering on the Iran–Iraq War." *Bulletin of the Atomic Scientists* (June 1987): 42–45.

Buckley, Peter J. *Studies in International Business*. New York: St. Martin's Press, 1992.

Bunton, John. "Western Contractors Face New Challenges." *Middle East Economic Digest* (MEED) (April 1979): 3–5.

Buzo, Adrian. *The Guerilla Dynasty: Politics and Leadership in North Korea*. London and New York: I.B. Tauris Publishers, 1999.

_____. *The Making of Modern Korea*, third edition. Abingdon and New York: Routledge, 2017.

Calabrese, John. "Japan in the Middle East." *The Pacific Review* 3 (1990): 100–112.

_____. "China and the Persian Gulf: Energy and Security." *Middle East Journal* 52, no. 3 (Summer 1998): 351–366.

Carafano, James Jay. "Implications of Iran Negotiations for North Korea." *The Journal of East Asian Affairs* 29, no. 2 (Fall/Winter 2015): 1–19.

Casey, Steven. *Selling the Korean War: Propaganda, Politics, and Public Opinion in the United States, 1950–1953*. New York: Oxford University Press, 2008.

Cathcart, Adam. "Kim Jong-Un Syndrome: North Korean Commemorative Culture and the Succession Process." In *Change and Continuity in North Korean Politics*, edited by Adam Cathcart, Robert Winstanley-Chesters, and Christopher K. Green. Abingdon and New York: Routledge, 2017.

Clarke, Richard A. *The Scorpion's Gate*. New York: The Penguin Putnam Inc., 2005.

Cook, Steven A. *False Dawn: Protest, Democracy, and Violence in the New Middle East*. New York: Oxford University Press, 2017.

Cooley, John K. "China and the Palestinians." *Journal of Palestine Studies* I, no. 2 (Winter 1972): 19–34.

Cooper, Andrew S. *The Oil Kings: How the U.S., Iran, and Saudi Arabia Changed the Balance of Power in the Middle East*. New York: Simon & Schuster Paperbacks, 2011.

Copper, John F. "Chinese Objectives in the Middle East." *China Report* 5 (January–February 1969): 8–13.

_____. *Taiwan: Nation-State or Province?*, third edition. Boulder, Colorado: Westview Press, 1999.

Cremer, Rolf D., and Mary J. Willes. *The Tongue of the Tiger: Overcoming Language Barriers in International Trade*. Singapore: World Scientific Publishing Co., 1998.

Davidson, Christopher M. *The Persian Gulf and Pacific Asia: From Indifference to Interdependence*. London: Hurst & Company, 2010.

Denney, Steven, Christopher Green, and Adam Cathcart. "Kim Jong-un and the Practice of Songun Politics." In *Change and Continuity in North Korean Politics*, edited by Adam Cathcart, Robert Winstanley-Chesters, and Christopher K. Green. Abingdon and New York: Routledge, 2017.

Dent, Christopher M. *The Foreign Economic Policies of Singapore, South Korea and Taiwan*. Cheltenham, UK: Edward Elgar, 2002.

Dore, Ronald. "Japan in the Coming Century: Looking East or West?" In *Japan's Role in International Politics since World War II*, edited by Edward R. Beauchamp. New York and London: Garland Publishing, 1998.

Dowty, Alan. "Japan and the Middle East: Signs of Change?" *Middle East Review of International Affairs* 4 (2000): 67–76.

Eberstadt, Nicholas. *The North Korea Economy: Between Crisis and Catastrophe*. New Brunswick, NJ: Transaction Publishers, 2009.

Ehrhardt, George. "Japan between the United States and the Middle East." In *Strategic Interests in the Middle East: Opposition and Support for US Foreign Policy*, edited by Jack Covarrubias, and Tom Lansford. Hampshire, England and Burlington, US: Ashgate, 2007.

Engel, Jeffrey A. ed. *The China Diary of George H.W. Bush: The Making of a Global President*. Princeton, NJ: Princeton University Press, 2008.

Field, Graham. *Economic Growth and Political Change in Asia*. New York: St. Martin's Press, 1995.

Fisher, Richard D. *China's Military Modernization: Building for Regional and Global Reach*. Westport, CT: Praeger Security International, 2008.

Foley, Michael. *Political Leadership: Themes, Contexts, and Critiques*. New York: Oxford University Press, 2013.

Ford, Christopher A. *The Mind of Empire: China's History and Modern Foreign Relations*. Lexington, KY: The University Press of Kentucky, 2010.

French, Howard W. *China's Second Continent: How a Million Migrants Are Building a New Empire in Africa*. New York: Alfred A. Knopf, 2014.

____. *Everything under the Heavens: How the Past Helps Shape China's Push for Global Power*. New York: Alfred A. Knopf, 2017.

French, Paul. *North Korea: The Paranoid Peninsula – A Modern History*. London and New York: Zed Books, 2005.

____. *Our Supreme Leader: The Making of Kim Jong-un*. London: Zed Books, 2016.

Fuller, Douglas B. "Taiwan's Industrial Policies for High-technology Sectors 1975–2012." In *Technology Transfer between the US, China and Taiwan: Moving Knowledge*, edited by Douglas B. Fuller, Murray A. Rubinstein. Abingdon and New York: Routledge, 2013.

Geldenhuys, Deon. *Isolated States: A Comparative Analysis*. New York: The Press Syndicate of the University of Cambridge, 1990.

Gertz, Bill. *The China Threat: How the People's Republic Targets America.* Washington, D.C.: Regnery Publishing, 2000.

_____. *The Failure Factory: How Unelected Bureaucrats, Liberal Democrats, and Big Government Republicans are Undermining America's Security and Leading US to War.* New York: Crown Forum, 2008.

Gill, Bates, and James Reilly. "The Tenuous Hold of China Inc. in Africa." *The Washington Quarterly* 30, no. 3 (Summer 2007): 37–52.

Gilley, Bruce, and Andrew O'Neil. "China's Rise through the Prism of Middle Powers." In *Middle Powers and the Rise of China*, edited by Bruce Gilley, and Andrew O'Neil. Washington, D.C.: Georgetown University Press, 2014.

Goldstein, Jonathan. ed. *China and Israel, 1948–1998: A Fifty Year Retrospective.* Westport, CT: Praeger, 1999.

_____. *Jewish Identities in East and Southeast Asia: Singapore, Manila, Taipei, Harbin, Shanghai, Rangoon, and Surabaya.* Berlin and Boston: De Gruyter Oldenbourg, 2015.

Gonzalez, Nathan. *Engaging Iran: The Rise of a Middle East Powerhouse and America's Strategic Choice.* Westport, CT: Praeger, 2007.

Grayson, James H. *Korea: A Religious History.* New York: RoutledgeCurzon, 2002.

Grinberg, Nicolas. "From Miracle to Crisis and Back: The Political Economy of South Korean Long-Term Development." *Journal of Contemporary Asia* 44, no. 4 (2014): 711–734.

Haass, Richard. *War of Necessity, War of Choice: A Memoir of Two Iraq Wars.* New York: Simon & Schuster, 2009.

Haggard, Stephan, and Marcus Noland. *Famine in North Korea: Markets, Aid, and Reform.* New York: Columbia University Press, 2007.

Harding, Harry. *China's Second Revolution: Reform after Mao.* Washington, D.C.: The Brookings Institution, 1987.

Hart, Gary. *The Fourth Power: A Grand Strategy for the United States in the Twenty-First Century.* New York: Oxford University Press, 2004.

Hartung, William D. "U.S.–Korea Jet Deal Boosts Arms Trade." *Bulletin of the Atomic Scientists* 46, no. 9 (1990): 18–24.

Hayes, Louis D. *Japan and the Security of Asia.* Lanham, MA: Lexington Books, 2001.

Hein, Patrick. "Leadership and Nationalism: Assessing Shinzo Abe." In *Asian Nationalisms Reconsidered*, edited by Jeff Kingston. Abingdon and New York: Routledge, 2016.

Henderson, Jeffrey. *East Asian Transformation: On the Political Economy of Dynamism, Governance and Crisis.* Abingdon and New York: Routledge, 2011.

Hess, Gary R. *Presidential Decisions for War: Korea, Vietnam, and the Persian Gulf.* Baltimore, MD: The Johns Hopkins University Press, 2001.

Hickey, Dennis Van Vranken. *Foreign Policy Making in Taiwan: From Principle to Pragmatism.* Abingdon and New York: Routledge, 2007.

Hilton, Mark. *Restrained Trade: Cartels in Japan's Basic Materials Industries.* Ithaca and London: Cornell University Press, 1996.

Howard, Roger. *Iran in Crisis?: The Future of the Revolutionary Regime and the US Response.* London and New York: Zed Books Ltd, 2004.

Hundt, David. "Economic Crisis in Korea and the Degraded Developmental State." *Australian Journal of International Affairs* 68, no. 5 (2014): 499–514.

Hunsberger, Warren S. "Japan's International Role, Past, Present, and Prospective." In *Japan's Quest: The Search for International Role, Recognition, and Respect,* edited by Warren S. Hunsberger. Armonk, NY: M.E. Sharpe, 1997.

Hyde, Martin, and Anthony Hyde. *Going to University Abroad: A Guide to Studying Outside the UK.* Abingdon and New York: Routledge, 2014.

Ikeuchi, Satoshi. *Chūtō kiki no shingen wo yomu* [Reading the Epicenter of Middle East Crisis]. Tokyo: Shinchosha, 2009.

International Business Publications USA. *Taiwan: National Security and Defense Law Handbook,* fourth edition. Washington, D.C.: International Business Publications USA, 2008.

International Monetary Fund. *United Arab Emirates: 2002 Article IV Consultation-Staff Country Reports.* Washington, D.C.: International Monetary Fund, 2003.

_____. *United Arab Emirates: Selected Issues and Statistical Appendix.* Washington, D.C.: International Monetary Fund, 2003.

Jacobs, J. Bruce. "One China, Diplomatic Isolation and a Separate Taiwan." In *China's Rise, Taiwan's Dilemma's and International Peace,* edited by Edward Friedman. Abingdon and New York: Routledge, 2006.

Jacobs, Justin M. *Xinjiang and the Modern Chinese State.* Seattle: University of Washington Press, 2016.

Jones Bruce, and David Steven. *The Risk Pivot: Great Powers, International Security, and the Energy Revolution.* Washington, D.C.: Brookings Institute Press, 2015.

Juneau, Thomas, and Sam Razavi. *Iranian Foreign Policy since 2001: Alone in the World.* Abingdon and New York: Routledge, 2013.

Kaplan, Robert D. *The Revenge of Geography: What the Map Tells Us About Coming Conflicts and the Battle against Fate.* New York: Random House, 2012.

_____. *The Return of Marco Polo's World: War, Strategy, and American Interests in the Twenty-first Century.* New York: Random House Publishing Group, 2018.

Klare, Michael T. *American Arms Supermarket.* Austin: University of Texas Press, 1984.

Lampton, David M. *Following the Leader: Ruling China, from Deng Xiaoping to Xi Jinping.* Berkeley and Los Angeles, CA: University of California Press, 2014.

Large, Daniel. "Beyond 'Dragon in the Bush': The Study of China–Africa Relations." *African Affairs* 107, no. 426 (2008): 45–61.

Leibo, Steven A. *East and Southeast Asia: The World Today Series 2017–2018.* Lanham, MD: Stryker–Post Publications, 2017.

Lilley, Peter. *Dirty Dealing: The Untold Truth about Global Money Laundering, International Crime and Terrorism.* London and Philadelphia: Kogan Page, 2006.

Marchetti, Victor, and John D. Marks. *The CIA and the Cult of Intelligence.* New York: Knopf, 1974.

Mark, Craig. *The Abe Restoration: Contemporary Japanese Politics and Reformation.* Lanham, MD: Lexington Books, 2016.

Mathews, Gordon. *Ghetto at the Center of the World: Chungking Mansions, Hong Kong.* Chicago and London: The University of Chicago Press, 2011.

McEachern, Patrick. *Inside the Red Box: North Korea's Post-Totalitarian Politics.* New York: Columbia University Press, 2010.

McNally, Christopher A. "Reflections on Capitalism and China's Emergent Political Economy." In *China's Emergent Political Economy: Capitalism in the Dragon's Lair,* edited by Christopher A. McNally. Abingdon and New York: Routledge, 2008.

Meinardus, Ronald. "Anti-Americanism in Korea and Germany: Comparative Perspectives." In *Korean Attitudes toward the United States: Changing Dynamics,* edited by David I. Steinberg. Armonk, NY: M.E. Sharpe, 2005.

Miller, Tom. *China's Asian Dream: Empire Building along the New Silk Road.* London: Zed Books, 2017.

Mills, Lawrence. *Protecting Free Trade: The Hong Kong Paradox 1947–1997.* Hong Kong: Hong Kong University Press, 2012.

Millward, James A. *The Silk Road: A Very Short Introduction.* New York: Oxford University Press, 2013.

Ministry of Defense. *Defense of Japan 2007.* Tokyo: Ministry of Defense, Annual White Paper, 2007.

Ministry of Foreign Affairs (the Republic of Korea). *Wegyo Munseo* [Diplomatic Archives]. Seoul: Ministry of Foreign Affairs, 1996.

———. *Diplomatic White Paper 2015.* Seoul: MOFA, 2015.

———. *Diplomatic White Paper 2016.* Seoul: MOFA, 2016.

Moran, Michael. *The Reckoning: Debt, Democracy, and the Future of American Power.* New York: Palgrave Macmillan, 2012.

Nathan Andrew J., and Andrew Scobell. *China's Search for Security.* New York: Columbia University Press, 2012.

Natsios, Andrew S. *The Great North Korean Famine: Famine, Politics, and Foreign Policy.* Washington, D.C.: United States Institute of Peace, 2001.

Navias, Martin S., and E. R. Hooton. *Tanker Wars: The Assault on Merchant Shipping during the Iran–Iraq Conflict, 1980–1988.* London and New York: I.B. Tauris, 1996.

Nihon Boeki Shinkokai. *China Newsletter*, Volumes 49–65. Tokyo: Nihon Boeki Shinkokai, 1984.

Office of Technology Assessment. *Technology Transfer to the Middle East*, Publication no. OTA-ISC-173. Washington, D.C.: Office of Technology Assessment, U.S. Government Printing Office, 1984.

Ōnishi, Madoka. *Iran keizai wo kaibō suru* [Scrutinizing Iranian Economy]. Tokyo: JETRO, 2000.

O'Reilly, Marc J. *Unexceptional: America's Empire in the Persian Gulf, 1941–2007.* Lanham, MD: Lexington Books, 2008.

Penn, Michael. *Japan and the War on Terror: Military Force and Political Pressure in the US–Japanese Alliance.* London and New York: I.B. Tauris, 2014.

Phillips, David L. *An Uncertain Ally: Turkey under Erdogan's Dictatorship.* Abingdon and New York: Routledge, 2017.

Pirie, Iain, "The New Korean Political Economy: Beyond the Models of Capitalism Debate." *The Pacific Review* 25, no. 3 (2012): 365–386.

———. "Korea and the Global Economic Crisis." *The Pacific Review* 29, no. 5, (2016): 671–692.

Polk, William R. *Understanding Iran: Everything You Need to Know, from Persia to the Islamic Republic, from Cyrus to Ahmadinejad.* New York: Palgrave Macmillan, 2009.

Pritchard, Charles L. *Failed Diplomacy: The Tragic Story of How North Korea Got the Bomb.* Washington, D.C.: Brookings Institution Press, 2007.

Radtke, Kurt W. "Japan–Israel Relations in the Eighties." *Asian Survey* 28, no. 5 (May 1988): 526–540.

Ravenal, Earl C. "Approaching China, Defending Taiwan." *Foreign Affairs* 50, no. 1 (1971): 44–58.

Robertson, Jeffrey. *Diplomatic Style and Foreign Policy: A Case Study of South Korea*. Abingdon and New York: Routledge, 2016.

Ross, Michael L. *The Oil Curse: How Petroleum Wealth Shapes the Development of Nations*. Princeton and Oxford: Princeton University Press, 2012.

Rubin, Barry. "The Persian Gulf amid Global and Regional Crises." In *Crises in the Contemporary Persian Gulf*, edited by Barry Rubin. New York: Frank Cass Publishers, 2002.

Rubinstein, Murray A. "The Evolution of Taiwan's Economic Miracle 1945–2000: Personal Accounts and Political Narratives." In *Technology Transfer between the US, China and Taiwan: Moving Knowledge*, edited by Douglas B. Fuller, and Murray A. Rubinstein. Abingdon and New York: Routledge, 2013.

Russell, Richard L. *Weapons Proliferation and War in the Greater Middle East: Strategic Contest*. Abingdon and New York: Routledge, 2005.

Ryan, Michael P. *Playing By the Rules: American Trade Power and Diplomacy in the Pacific*. Washington, D.C.: Georgetown University Press, 1995.

Sagan, Scott, Kenneth N. Waltz, and Richard K. Betts. "A Nuclear Iran: Promoting Stability or Courting Disaster?" *Journal of International Affairs* 60, no. 2 (Spring 2007): 135–50.

Salus, Bill. *Nuclear Showdown in Iran: Revealing the Ancient Prophecy of Elam*. La Quinta, CA: Prophecy Depot Ministries, 2014.

Saxer, Carl J. "Democratization, Globalization and the Linkage of Domestic and Foreign Policy in South Korea." *The Pacific Review* 26, no. 2 (2013): 177–198.

Schwekendiek, Daniel J. *South Korea: A Socioeconomic Overview from the Past to Present*. Abingdon and New York: Routledge, 2017.

Shindler, Colin. ed. *Israel and the World Powers: Diplomatic Alliances and International Relations beyond the Middle East*. London and New York: I.B. Tauris, 2014.

Simpfendorfer, Ben. "The Impact of the Arab Revolutions on China's Foreign Policy." In *The EU–China Relationship, European Perspectives – A Manual for Policy Makers, edited by* Brown Kerry. London: Imperial College Press, 2015.

Soysal, Ismail. *Soguk Savas Donemi ve Turkiye: Olaylar Kronolojisi (1945–1975)* [The Cold War Period and Turkey: Chronology of Events (1945–1975)]. Istanbul: ISIS Yayincilik, 1997.

Stockholm International Peace Research Institute (SIPRI). *The Arms Trade with the Third World*. New York: Holmes & Meier Publishers, 1975.

Sutter, Robert G. *The United States and Asia: Regional Dynamics and Twenty-First-Century Relations*. Lanham, MD: Rowman & Littlefield, 2015.

____. *U.S. Policy toward China: An Introduction to the Role of Interest Groups.* Lanham, MD: Rowman & Littlefield, 1998.

Sweeney, John. *North Korea Undercover: Inside the World's Most Secret State.* New York: Pegasus Books, 2015.

Taiwan Bureau of Energy. *Energy Statistics Handbook 2010.* Taipei: Taiwan Bureau of Energy, Ministry of Economic Affairs, 2010.

Taylor, Jay. *The Generalissimo: Chiang Kai-shek and the Struggle for Modern China.* Cambridge, MA: Harvard University Press, 2000.

____. "Taiwan's Foreign Policy and Africa: The Limitations of Dollar Diplomacy." *Journal of Contemporary China* 11, no. 30 (2002): 125–140.

Tudor, Daniel, and James Pearson. *North Korea Confidential: Private Markets, Fashion Trends, Prison Camps, Dissenters and Defectors.* North Clarendon, VT: Tuttle Publishing, 2015.

Wallace, Robert Daniel. *North Korea and the Science of Provocation: Fifty Years of Conflict-Making.* Jefferson, NC: McFarland & Company, 2016.

Wolf, Charles Jr., and Norman D. Levin. *Modernizing the North Korean System: Objectives, Method, and Application.* Santa Monica, CA: Rand, 2008.

Woodman, Georg. *Cultural Shock-Taiwan: Cow Mentality, Rubber Slipper Fashion in BinLang Country.* Philadelphia, PA: Xlibris Corporation, 2010.

Woolley, Peter J. *Japan's Navy: Politics and Paradox, 1971–2000.* Boulder, CO: Lynne Rienner Publishers, 2000.

Worringer, Renée. ed. *The Islamic Middle East and Japan: Perceptions, Aspirations, and the Birth of Intra-Asian Modernity.* Princeton, NJ: Markus Wiener, 2007.

Worth, Richard. *Kim Jong Il.* New York: Chelsea House, 2008.

Yamauchi, Masayuki. *Sensō to gaikō: Iraku, amerika, nihon* [War and Diplomacy: Iraq, United States, Japan]. Daiamondosha, 2003.

Yomiuri Shinbun Seijibu. *Gaikō wo kenka ni shita otoko: Koizumi gaikō 2000 nichi no shinjitsu* [The Man Who Made Diplomacy a Fall-out: The Truth of 2000 Days of Koizumi Diplomacy]. Tokyo: Shinchō sha, 2006.

Yonhap News Agency. *North Korea Handbook.* Armonk, NY: M.E. Sharpe, 2003.

INDEX

Numerals

2030 Vision, 16, 44
9/11 incident, effect of, 47

A

Abe, Shinzo, 2, 37-52, 54-64, 76
Abenomics, 41, 44
administration, 12, 48, 68, 76, 82, 87, 102, 104, 106, 113
Africa, 7, 24, 32, 33, 41, 56, 59-62, 70, 87-89, 112, 118
agenda, 7, 8, 24, 37, 40, 44, 51, 88, 120, 138
Ahmadinejad, Mahmoud, 74, 100, 101, 134, 147
Air Koryo, 103
Al Jazeera, 74, 105, 137
al-Assad, Bashar, 29, 110
alliance system, 61, 70
ammunition, 113, 133
Ankara, 23, 25, 53-55, 81, 82, 108
Arab Spring, 28, 30-33, 61, 89
Arabic (language), 136
Arab–Israeli conflict, 124
Aramco, 44, 72, 143
arts exchanges, 149, 150
Asia, 1, 3, 4, 9, 18, 19, 24, 28, 31, 39, 41, 43, 45, 46, 49, 56, 58, 67, 68, 70,

72, 86, 94, 101, 106, 115, 119, 124, 127, 128, 137, 138, 141-145, 149, 150
Asian Infrastructure Investment Bank (AIIB), 34
Asian Tigers, 125
assassination, 69
Australia, 38, 107
autarky, 96
autonomous territory, 142
axis of evil, 106
Azadegan, 46

B

Ba'ath Party (Iraq), 105-107
Ba'ath Party (Syria), 29,
Baghdad, 21, 22, 50-52, 62, 105-107
Bahrain, 46, 74, 130, 144
Ban Ki-moon, 80
Barakah, 73
Barzani, Nechirvan, 51, 52
Beijing, 6, 9, 11-13, 15, 20-27, 29-35, 46, 99, 108, 120, 121, 123, 124, 132, 141, 147, 148
Bosphorus Bridge, 83
BRICS, 14, 34
brothers in blood, 81
Bush, George W., 32, 106, 119

C

D

E

F